LF

D1070995

Yale Western Americana Series, 15

California's Utopian Colonies

by

R O B E R T V . H I N E

New Haven and London
Yale University Press

Originally published in 1953 by the
Henry E. Huntington Library & Art Gallery
Copyright © 1966 by Yale University Press
Second printing, July 1969
Printed by the Carl Purington Rollins Printing-Office
of the Yale University Press,
New Haven, Connecticut

Distributed in Great Britain, Europe,
Asia, and Africa by Yale University
Press Ltd., London; in Canada by
McGill-Queen's University Press,
Montreal; and in Mexico by Centro
Interamericano de Libros Académicos,
Mexico City.

Library of Congress catalog card number: 53–9114

TO SHIRLEY

CONTENTS

vii

CHARTS

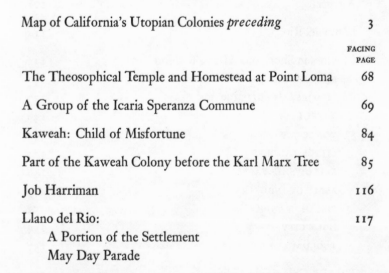

ILLUSTRATIONS

S INCE THE fifteenth century when Garcia Ordoñez de
Montalvo coined a new word, California, for an imagi-
nary island rich in pearls and gold, the name has called
up visions of utopia. Centuries afterward, applied to
Baja California and gradually to the vast, unexplored regions
northward, the term for the land of fertile coastal valleys and
rugged mountains continued to carry the hint of an earthly
paradise. It is hardly surprising that, even as late as the nineteenth
and twentieth centuries, attempts to reconstruct the Garden of
Eden should have flourished along the Western Sea.

Yet, curiously enough, the story of these utopian colonies in
California has been largely overlooked, and only a few have been
previously described. Several historical journals have treated the
Kaweah Colony near Visalia, and the Fountain Grove Colony
near Santa Rosa has been dealt with briefly in biographies of
Thomas Lake Harris and Laurence Oliphant. But the annals of
many of the utopias have passed into obscurity, and the collected
history of all the colonies in the state has never been written.

Thus, like an early map of virgin territory, this study is likely
to be incomplete. Undoubtedly other utopian colonies, which
are not included in this book, have been formed in California.
In general, too, because society has labeled them "lunatic fringe,"
little effort has been made to preserve the records of any of the
colonies, even the most important ones, and in the minds of many
Californians the sooner they have been forgotten, the better.
Consequently, the sources for most colonies tend to be scanty,
and probably much remains unearthed.

This book could hardly have been finished without the generous
assistance of the Henry E. Huntington Library, Dr. John E.
Pomfret, its Director, and Dr. Robert G. Cleland, administrator
of the Rockefeller-Huntington Trustee Fund for the "study of
the economic, social, and cultural development of the Southwest."
Dr. Cleland analyzed the entire work, and many of its felicities
are his while the defects remain my own. Dr. Pomfret and Dr.

Frederick B. Tolles of the Huntington Library also read large portions of the manuscript and offered productive suggestions.

A portion of this history served as a dissertation for the degree of Doctor of Philosophy in Yale University, and for those sections I must thank Professors David M. Potter and Ralph H. Gabriel for invaluable guidance. The resulting thesis received the George Washington Egleston Historical Prize at Yale for 1952.

Dr. Louis B. Wright, now Director of the Folger Shakespeare Library in Washington, first suggested the subject itself. His encouragement and that of Dr. John H. Kemble and Dr. John H. Gleason of Pomona College helped to inaugurate the study in 1948. The first fruit appeared as "A California Utopia: 1885-1890," in the *Huntington Library Quarterly* for August, 1948.

To the staffs of the State Library in Sacramento and the Bancroft Library at the University of California in Berkeley and, above all, the Huntington Library in San Marino, I offer my deepest thanks for countless services; and, in particular, to Mary Isabel Fry, Marion Chevalier, and Erwin Morkisch.

I am indebted to the following generous persons for interviews, letters, and helpful information: Mrs. Marion Tinling of Sacramento (who allowed me to read her unpublished manuscript on Icaria), John Way of Temple City, Mrs. F. E. Coulter of the Bowers Memorial Museum in Santa Ana, Walter Millsap of Los Angeles, Miss Grace Heilman of the University of California at Los Angeles, Emmett A. Greenwalt (whose dissertation on the Point Loma community has been invaluable), James A. Long, Miss Grace F. Knoche, and Mrs. Hazel Minot of Pasadena, Mrs. Pearl F. Dower, Miss Ella Vogtherr, and Mrs. Patricia L. Mallory of Halcyon, Gerald Geraldson of New York City, and his son, Lloyd S. Geraldson of Auburn, William E. Riker of Holy City, David Aaron of Los Angeles, Ranger Howard Stagner of Sequoia National Park, Miss Alice M. Dehay and her brother, Paul Dehay, of Cloverdale, Ernest Marchand of San Diego State College, Mrs. Albert L. Gauthier and Jules Gentry of Corning, Iowa, Mrs. Eva Bettannier Mitchell of Pasadena, Ardin D. Hotchkiss of Covina, Miss Grace Buck of Puente, Robert Boyd of Tracy, lately removed to British Columbia, Mrs. Julia Montgomery of San Ysidro, George Burleson and Paul Newey of Modesto, Wendell Kramer of New York City, Martin Litton of Los Angeles, James Cheek of Highland Park, and Siegfried Bechhold and George W. King of Santa Rosa. To all, my sincerest appreciation.

For my wife thanks seem futile beside her boundless devotion and long labor to make this utopian dream a reality.

MT. SHASTA

EUREKA

CLOVERDALE
1
2
3
SANTA ROSA ★ SACRAMENTO
4

5
SAN FRANCISCO 17
17 17
6 ● MODESTO
7
HOLY CITY
MONTEREY

8
● VISALIA

10
● SAN LUIS OBISPO BAKERSFIELD
9

11 12
LOS ANGELES
13
● SAN BERNARDINO
14
15 ● ANAHEIM

16
● SAN DIEGO
17

PACIFIC
OCEAN

N
W E
S

MORMONS TO
SAN BERNARDINO
1852

MODJESKA'S COLON
EN ROUTE
187

| ICARIA SPERANZA AND FOUNTAIN GROVE | KAWEAH 1885 | POINT LOMA 1900 | LLANO DEL RIO 1900 | TUOLUMNE FARMS 1945 |

A map of the world that does not include Utopia is not worth even glancing at, for it leaves out the one country at which humanity is always landing.

OSCAR WILDE (*The Soul of Man Under Socialism*)

1 Icaria Speranza
2 Altruria
3 Fountain Grove — *Still Stands*
4 Army of Industry
5 Winters Island
6 Tuolumne Farms
7 Holy City
8 Kaweah
9 Temple Home
10 Joyful
11 Pisgah Grande
12 Llano del Rio
13 San Bernardino
14 Fellowship Farm
15 Modjeska's Colony
16 Point Loma
17 Little Landers

CALIFORNIA'S UTOPIAN COLONIES

1850-1950

CHAPTER I

Westward the Course
of Utopia

ONE EVENT occasionally may symbolize a movement; one hour, epitomize the work of years. So it was in 1890 when a wooden bridge suddenly collapsed under the extra weight of a boiler-engine, and the machine crashed through the boards into the waters of an icy Sierra stream. Men looked back, incredulous, arms akimbo, uncertain of the next move. The water swirled around the wheels, and the bridge girders jutted hopelessly askew. The boiler was a part of utopia and it had gone awash; forces had conspired against its crossing. Perhaps the men who watched the mishap, members of the Kaweah Colony, one of California's most important utopian experiments, wondered momentarily at the future of the ideal society.

Many of their hopes lay with the engine in the river. Without the machinery, no lumber could be milled; without lumber, the colony could not succeed economically; without economic stability, prospects seemed black indeed.

But these were zealous men, reformers, seekers after the perfect state. A shattered bridge and a stalled engine were temporary obstacles at most. For the social reformer—and these utopians were part of a tradition which reached back to the birth of civilization —far greater difficulties have not dampened zeal. Through high water and over broken bridges, men with a similar hope have painstakingly, tirelessly searched for utopia. Some have maintained that philosophers must be kings in the ideal republic. Some have said that institutions affect the state more profoundly than

3

the men who govern or that the masses of mankind must re-align their hearts before either rulers or institutions can be perfected.

But whatever the philosophic approach, among all these groups there have been reformers who would advance their ideal by establishing pilot communities, utopian colonies, previews of the perfect state. Nineteenth-century America witnessed not the first historically, but certainly the most extensive rash of such experiments. Bathed in the essential optimism of an era, confident of social progress, unhampered by governmental censorship, and abetted by inexpensive and expansive land, the utopian colonist found in nineteenth-century America a fertile milieu. And in spite of changed conditions, the utopian psychology continues to spill over into our own times; deep in the twentieth century, Americans still abandon homes and traditional society for newer utopias.

If among the hundreds of these experiments the basic patterns of motivation and embodiment had recurred consistently, the problem of defining a utopian colony would be simple. Certain clusters of ideal communities, especially in the first half of the nineteenth century, drank from clearly definable sources, and thus we can pigeonhole groups of Owenite or Fourierist colonies. With the last half of the century, however, the thought patterns resulting in communitarian experiment became far more numerous. Marxism erupted beneath the milder evolutionary socialism; portions of the religious world, moved by industrialism and urbanization, produced a Social Gospel and a Christian Socialism; the excesses of the Gilded Age evoked convulsive outbursts from Single-taxer, Populist, and the Nationalist followers of Edward Bellamy; and all of these streams of protest ran at one time or another into a communitarian course. How then to define "utopian colony," a term which must include them all, from New Harmony in Indiana to Fairhope in Alabama, from the transcendentalism of Brook Farm in settled Massachusetts to the socialism of Kaweah in the wild foothills of the Sierra Nevada?

The expression "utopian" since the time of Thomas More has connoted unreality and impracticality. For the socialist it assumed additional distaste when Marx and Engels in the *Communist Manifesto* compared the fumblings of "utopian socialism" with the assured progress of "scientific socialism." But "utopian" also denotes an ideal to which men aspire, concrete and real to its proponents, though visionary to its detractors. In this sense it has no satisfactory substitute and will be used in this study with an emphasis on the ideal, rather than on hopeless impracticality.

A utopian colony, thus, consists of a group of people who are attempting to establish a new social pattern based upon a vision of the ideal society and who have withdrawn themselves from the community at large to embody that vision in experimental form. The purpose is usually to create a model which other colonies and eventually mankind in general will follow. The concept of withdrawal, an important element in the definition, eliminates those organizations which through co-operative effort seek to transform society by working from within: consumers' and self-help co-operatives, factory profit-sharing leagues, or even labor unions. These bodies lay some claim to utopianism, but they base their reforms on the possibility of slow change within the existing order rather than establishing a completely new pattern. Hence the groups which withdraw can be logically isolated from other elements in the history of social reform.

A utopian colony may be either religious or secular. The religious colony seeks a community life which fulfills the family relationship implied by the fatherhood of God and the brotherhood of man. The Shakers, the Moravians, the Perfectionists at Oneida, and, in California, the Theosophists at Point Loma or the Harrisites at Fountain Grove—all reflected this aspect of Christian ethical thought. Such religious groups usually follow a man or a revelation and believe themselves a chosen people. No outsider achieves membership until he affirms absolute faith in the new teachings. The secular colony, on the other hand, may proclaim the brotherhood of man but it requires no sectarian or religious test of its members. It conceives of communal life almost as an end in itself or as a utilitarian expedient to a human happiness which can be achieved in this life. Like the religious colony, it resents the discords and cross-purposes of the competitive society from which it withdraws, and, although imposing no religious proof, it does demand a firm belief in the co-operative way of life.

The extent to which all goods are held in common provides another classification of colonies, but a difficult one because of the infinitely varying degrees of communal ownership. The word "communism," as slippery and ambiguous a term as the twentieth century has appropriated, will be used here only in its simplest and most rudimentary meaning, that is, a system of social organization in which all property is publicly owned. The Shakers in the northeastern United States most clearly illustrate a purely communistic utopia. Such colonies were not concerned with violent overthrow of governments or with the various totalitarian ideas associated with modern use of the word. Communism for them meant simply community rather than individual ownership.

All of the California colonies possessed some degree of communal holding, whether thoroughly socialistic or merely co-operative, but few approached the Shakers in unadulterated communism. Instead, most of the California groups followed a socialistic pattern, in which all means of production—machinery, raw materials, and community buildings—were normally owned in common, as at Kaweah, Llano, and Icaria Speranza. Individuals, however, could maintain private holdings outside of the colony and were not forced to deposit all their worldly belongings in the common fund. A few of the California utopias were merely co-operative, like the Theosophists at Point Loma, and permitted individual ownership of personal objects, including houses within the colony, but proscribed speculation, produced co-operatively, and shared a common social and intellectual life.

From 1850 to 1950 California witnessed the formation of a larger number of utopian colonies than any other state in the Union.[1] In this period at least seventeen groups embarked on an

[1]This statement needs qualification. Though I have examined the California records, I have not done so for every region. In composing lists of colonies in other states I have relied on such published compilations as Ralph Albertson

idealistic community experiment in California. Of these, six were religious and eleven secular.[2] This number includes only those which can reasonably be defined as utopian, although a whole area of peripheral cases exists.

Along this borderline, a large number of California settlements were co-operative in their inception but used the co-operative scheme only as a means to buy, develop, and move themselves to the land. Once this end was accomplished, all traces of communal life were abandoned. Such a method has been particularly prevalent in southern California where the problems of water development have been great enough to require group rather than individual capital. Anaheim, a familiar example, resulted from co-operative effort on the part of German artisans of San Francisco. In 1857 they pooled sufficient cash to send south one of their members, George Hansen, to buy land suitable for grape culture. None of them could afford, or at least did not wish to risk, the long, nonproductive period of developing irrigation, cultivating, and planting prior to the first harvest. So Hansen,

---

"A Survey of Mutualistic Communities in America," *Iowa Journal of History and Politics*, XXXIV (Oct., 1936), 375-444; Frederick A. Bushee, "Communistic Societies in the United States," *Political Science Quarterly*, XX (Dec., 1905), 625-64; "Co-operative Productive Enterprises in the United States," *Monthly Labor Review*, XLVII (Nov., 1938), 991-1000; Joseph Eaton and Saul Katz, *Research Guide on Co-operative Group Farming* (N.Y., 1942); Helen D. Jones, *Communal Settlements in the United States* (Washington, D.C., 1947); Alexander Kent, "Co-operative Communities in the United States," U. S. Dept. of Labor, *Bulletin*, XXXV (July, 1901), 563-646. These contain more extensive lists or charts than do the standard works such as Charles Gide, *Communist and Co-operative Colonies* (London, 1930), or William A. Hinds, *American Communities* (3rd ed., Chicago, 1908). Charles Nordhoff and John Humphrey Noyes both wrote too early to be of help in such a compilation. On the basis of these lists, in the period between 1850 and about 1940, New York, Wisconsin, and Washington had a number nearest to that in California, each with three colonies.

[2] The *religious*: Fountain Grove, Point Loma, Temple Home, Pisgah Grande, Holy City, and the Mormons at San Bernardino. The *secular*: Icaria Speranza, Kaweah, Altruria, Llano, Madame Modjeska's Farm, Joyful, Winters Island, Little Landers, Fellowship Farm, Army of Industry, and Tuolumne Farms. Little Landers, listed as one, actually as a movement produced several separate colonies. Kitsiookla is not included because of its temporary nature preparatory to a move to Canada; nor is Societas Fraternia, because, in the scantiness of material, it is difficult to identify its ideals; nor is Topolobampo, because it was located in Mexico, although its repercussions in California were considerable.

CHRONOLOGICAL CHART OF THE CALIFORNIA UTOPIAS

1850 1860 1870 1880 1890 1900 1910 1920 1930 1940 1950

MORMONS (San Bernardino)
FOUNTAIN GROVE
MODJESKA'S FARM
ICARIA SPERANZA
JOYFUL
KAWEAH
WINTERS ISLAND
ALTRURIA
POINT LOMA
TEMPLE HOME
LITTLE LANDERS
FELLOWSHIP FARM
LLANO
ARMY OF INDUSTRY
PISGAH GRANDE
HOLY CITY
TUOLUMNE FARMS

RELIGIOUS
SECULAR

hiring inexpensive Mexican labor, spent the better part of two years installing water systems and setting out trees, vines, and windbreaks. The owners of the land did not move south until this work was finished and a harvest ready to be garnered. Upon arriving, the settlers divided the land by lot, each assumed full title to his own tract, and the co-operative nature of the enterprise ceased.

Another type of colony in California possessed certain vague communal features but based its group living not on social ideals, but on congenial beliefs or on common backgrounds. The Rosicrucians at Oceanside and the Presbyterians at Westminster gathered by reason of encompassing ideas. Common national backgrounds cemented the Danes at Solvang and two English settlements as well, one in the Burns Valley near Clear Lake and the other at Rosedale near Bakersfield. All of these colonies can be excluded from the utopian category because their ideals have been other than social or because their reasons for living communally have included no conscious message for the outside world.

Although California seems rich in utopian experiments, it should be remembered that the period of preponderance in California is not the time in which utopias blossomed profusely east of the Mississippi. A few decades in the first half of the nineteenth century probably saw more colonies in New York or Massachusetts, for example, than the whole period from 1850 to 1950. In the earlier years the Shaker and Fourierist colonies alone would outnumber all of California's utopias. But Fourierism and Shakerism, to say nothing of Owenism, flourished too early for California to participate. In the late nineteenth century, California underwent, however, phases of population growth and industrial expansion which were roughly analogous to the early nineteenth century in the north Atlantic states. This tardy development may be a partial explanation for the large numbers of later California colonies.

Unlike many states, California experienced unusually vigorous bursts of population growth—the Gold Rush, the boom of the 1880's in the southern counties, and the boom of the 1920's throughout the state. Personal roots in the community had little time to develop before being disturbed by the next onrush, and the population consequently remained to a large extent heterogeneous and fluid. Furthermore, the climate attracted a large percentage of retired and elderly persons who, with idle minds and lives, were frequently led into panaceas like the Townsend Plan. The southern part of the state was notoriously transient. Carey McWilliams estimated that for the twenty-five years following 1920 Los Angeles alone counted annually 200,000 temporary residents.[3]

The nature of the population, however, though it may be basic in explaining other aspects of California life, is a most inadequate explanation for the number of utopian colonies in California. It would only apply to those communities which had indigenous founders or followers, such as Altruria, Kaweah, or Llano; yet these experiments represented only one aspect of national movements, like Christian Socialism or secular, political socialism. More aberrant colonies, those which flowered from doctrines which did not root deeply in American life—Theosophy at Point Loma or Respirationism at Fountain Grove—were founded in other parts of the country and moved their memberships more or less bodily to the Pacific coast.

Obviously the same factors which stimulated so rapid a growth in population during the American Period in California likewise drew utopian colonies. Mild climate and fertility of soil provided attractive foundations, lavishly advertised by railroads, promoters, and chambers of commerce. Letters and word-of-mouth descriptions further focused California on the mind of the nation as a likely spot for utopian experiment. Thus, when young Alexis Marchand at Cloverdale, California, wrote his friends in Iowa of the blossoming valley and warm sunshine of his newly found

---

[3]*Southern California Country* (N.Y., 1946), p. 258. For figures regarding age and nature of the population see State of California, Dept. of Education, *Occupational Trends in California with Implications for Vocational Education: Nature of the Population* (Sacramento, Calif., 1937); also U. S. Bureau of the Census, *Fourteenth Census of the United States, 1920: Bulletin, Population: California, Composition and Characteristics of the Population* (Washington, D.C., 1921).

Icarian Eden, he played the part of a good California salesman, as well as a utopian, in calling his comrades to the promised land. And Albert Shaw, the historian of Icaria, succumbed to the same lure when he admitted that "if the writer were seeking the realization of a Utopia, ... of all places and all occupations on earth he would choose as most consonant with the theories and purposes of communism—California and horticulture."[4]

[4]Shaw, *Icaria* (N.Y., 1884), p. 142.

CHAPTER 2

Fountain Grove

I N THE EARLY SUMMER of 1875 construction began on a commodious, dignified Adams-Georgian home in a secluded foothill valley two miles north of Santa Rosa. The grounds were planted "after the style of an English park . . . including lakes and fountains," and the local paper happily predicted that the expenditure would total between $40,000 and $50,000.[1] The impressive residence, finished in November, was designed, along with numerous other buildings on hundreds of surrounding acres, to shelter the Brotherhood of the New Life and its primate, Thomas Lake Harris. A fountain in the midst of eucalyptus and fruit groves provided both the name, Fountain Grove, and the setting for a communism echoing John Humphrey Noyes, Emanuel Swedenborg, and, faintly, Edward Bellamy.

Thomas Lake Harris was throughout his life a religious mystic and a poet; his voluminous writings never drifted far from either shore.[2] But, like Orestes Brownson, the New England clergyman, he was theologically a vagabond. Born in 1823 in England and emigrating with his parents to Utica, New York, at the age of five, he was raised in a strict Calvinist home. This atmosphere plus an unhappy relationship with his stepmother caused his revolt from family and Calvinism. He became a Universalist, studying its theology as a homeless youth of eighteen and holding in his early twenties Universalist pulpits in the Mohawk Valley and New York City.

During the late 1840's, while Kate and Margaret Fox per-

---

[1] *Sonoma Democrat* (Santa Rosa, Calif.), July 31, 1875.

[2] For a brief biography see Herbert W. Schneider, "Thomas Lake Harris," *DAB;* for more extensive treatment, Herbert W. Schneider and George Lawton, *A Prophet and a Pilgrim* (N.Y., 1942), hereafter cited as Schneider.

formed their "spirit rappings" and Americans generally became increasingly conscious of mediums and trances, Harris moved from Universalism into spiritualism. He followed fiery, young Andrew Jackson Davis until Davis became involved in free-love scandals which alienated Harris. The spiritualist teachings, nevertheless, provided Harris with his first experience as a communitarian, through participation in a psychical community experiment at Mountain Cove, Virginia, from 1850 to 1853. Spiritualism at this time preached social reconstruction as a handmaiden to spiritual regeneration. But Harris' mind was not content with the seance table as the foundation for social reform. He had begun reading the eighteenth-century mystic philosopher Emanuel Swedenborg and here he found a marriage of Christianity with spiritualism which pleased him. He remained a spiritualist, believing in direct communication with the dead, for the remainder of his life; but from the circumscribed cult of spiritualism he ranged into wider fields.

In retrospect Swedenborgianism, Harris' next faith, was a logical step. It enabled him to retain his earlier Calvinist ethic and a vivid, substantial heaven and hell; but at the same time it allowed him a kinder, Universalist view of man's goodness; and, still more important, it admitted spiritualism to a prominent place. Almost all of Harris' later teachings can be traced to one or a combination of these strains, and more particularly to their union in Swedenborg. Harris pictured a Golden Age in the past succeeded by an increasing gulf between God and Man; Swedenborg wrote of an early era of human perfection when men had intercourse with angels, followed by a change wherein "heaven removed itself from man, and this more and more, even to the present age."[3] Harris spoke of "counterparts," with whom man sought spiritual union; Swedenborg postulated a "conjugial love," a relationship achieved by means of a "correspondence" or image of the human body in the immortal soul.[4] Both hypothesized and per-

[3]Emanuel Swedenborg, *Arcana Coelestia* (12 vols., N.Y., 1938), X, 40.

[4]Swedenborg, *The Delights of Wisdom Pertaining to Conjugial Love* (N.Y., 1938).

sonally experienced an internal awakening through which men penetrated directly to truth and God. Both revolted against institutionalism, yet each was responsible for establishing a sect of his own.

Even more important to the story of Fountain Grove is the effect of Swedenborg on Harris' social thought. By Harris' time the followers of Swedenborg were divided between those more interested in the spiritualistic arcana and those concerned with the social message in Swedenborgianism. Harris, like Philip Freneau before him, discovered in Swedenborg "the noblest system to reform mankind."[5] Swedenborgians, with Quakers, had led the anti-slavery movement of the eighteenth century; Swedenborgians were among the leaders of the nineteenth-century American temperance crusade. Some Swedenborgians had even interpreted their leader's social gospel to mean communism. In America this position was taken chiefly by German immigrants who at Yellow Springs and Cincinnati, Ohio, and Jasper, Iowa, established communistic settlements on Swedenborgian principles. Just as the Brook Farm disciples and men like Henry James, Sr., had assimilated Swedenborg along with Fourier, these groups felt the similarities between Fourier's "passional principle" and Swedenborg's "conjugial love" as bases for the brotherhood of man.[6]

In the mid-1850's Harris ministered near Washington Square in New York City to a congregation of Swedenborgians, but his theological wanderings were not over. He had revolted in turn from his home, from Calvinism, from Universalism, and partially from spiritualism; his dissent from Swedenborgianism might have been predicted. The beginnings of the schism can be traced to 1857 when he received a series of mystical revelations including that of Divine Respiration, a supernatural method of breathing enabling man to commune directly with God. Harris was immediately denounced by the Swedenborgian parent organization and

[5] *The Poems of Philip Freneau* (3 vols., Princeton, 1902-07), II, 307.

[6] Charles A. Hawley, "Swedenborgianism and the Frontier," *Church History*, VI (Sept., 1937), 211, 213-17.

the following year left his New York congregation to sail for England with his new revelations. One whole year of his absence was spent in Scotland, and in Glasgow he gathered around him the first nucleus of the Brotherhood of the New Life, Harris' final metamorphosis from Swedenborgianism. While lecturing and traveling in the British Isles, he gained converts to his new brotherhood and interested sympathizers like the Ruxton family, who were later to help finance his community ventures. Nevertheless, disappointed that Scots and Englishmen did not rally to his standard in the numbers he had expected, and feeling, with the outbreak of the Civil War, that America required his healing presence, he returned to the United States, fired with two new plans: the expansion of his group into a universal brotherhood and the realization of this aim through communitarian living.

Harris organized thereafter four colonies for members of the New Life. To Wassaic, a hamlet in Dutchess County, New York, he led in 1861 a handful of his former Swedenborgian parishioners, including Jane Lee Waring and Mr. and Mrs. James Requa. As new members joined, a more extensive property was purchased a few miles up the valley at Amenia. The brotherhood at Amenia numbered about thirty-five when it was invigorated by the arrival of two of Harris' most distinguished converts, Lady Oliphant and her son, Laurence.[7] On admission the Oliphants contributed sufficient money to justify further expansion, and the community thereupon moved during late 1867 and early 1868 to Brocton, New York, on the shores of Lake Erie. The experiment now numbered at least seventy-five.[8]

---

[7] The story of Laurence Oliphant and his relations with Harris is amazingly colorful. Before meeting Harris, Oliphant, the young Englishman, had been an adventurer in India and Russia, a journalist, satirist, novelist, and private secretary of Lord Elgin on several important diplomatic missions. In 1865 he fulfilled one of his personal ambitions by election to Parliament, but within two years he and his mother had sacrificed all their social advantages and joined Harris in the community at Amenia. For brief sketch see Sir Leslie Stephen, "Laurence Oliphant (1829-88)," *DNB*. For more extensive treatment see Schneider.

[8] Schneider, pp. 147-50. W. P. Swainson, *Thomas Lake Harris and His Occult Teaching* (London, 1922), p. 13, refers to sixty adults, besides children, who settled at Brocton.

The Brotherhood of the New Life was thus the product of ecclesiastical revolt, a deep feeling for social reform, Christianity, spiritualism, and Swedenborgianism mixed in the mind of Harris with later additions of Oriental mysticism and late nineteenth-century anti-monopoly socialism. It proclaimed a "pivotal man," Thomas Lake Harris, within whom the cosmic forces of good and evil battled for predominance on a physical plane. Christ would appear again on earth, but His coming would be announced through the pivotal personality. The concept of the primate or pivotal man worked on Harris' mind until he came eventually to associate, if not identify, himself with Christ. God was conceived as bisexual and Christ revealed himself as the Divine Man-Woman, a concept too precious and advanced to have been disclosed while He ministered in Galilee. Through sex, in its purely spiritual aspects, man came closest to God. Harris exposed the nature of a Divine Breath or Respiration which, when properly cultivated by man, would protect him from all evil and lift him to the very threshold of heaven.

No small part of the appeal of the brotherhood came from the personality of Harris himself, a slender, pale man with massive eyebrows overhanging penetrating eyes, with a patriarchal beard, and with a resonant, powerful voice.[9] Even his prose reflected a richly imaginative mind, and Edwin Markham, the California poet and long a friend of Harris, called his poetry "musical in flow, and often beautiful in diction."[10] His imagery was heavily sensuous, as the following passages suggest.

> Girls, my girls, pure passion-roses,
> In you I have bled:
> In you all my life reposes,—
> Bridal wreath and bed.
>
> .   .   .   .   .   .

---

[9] For a vivid eye-witness account of Harris preaching to his Independent Christian congregation in New York, see J. Parton, *The Life of Horace Greeley* (N.Y., 1854), pp. 425-27.

[10] *California the Wonderful* (N.Y., 1914), p. 343.

> I clasped her,—could I help it? and she caught
> My form and whirled me in the rapid stress
> Of music, sweet as love and swift as thought;
> But when still more I sought to wreathe and press
> Her warm, white shape of gliding loveliness,
> She coyly drew and beckoned to the dance.
> Not much of dead religion I profess,
> But living godliness shone by her glance,
> And in its light I met the Infinite Advance.[11]

One of Harris' devoted followers said of his poetry that Shakespeare, Milton, and Dante were all right in their time, "but hark to the glad new voice."[12]

In 1875 Harris transferred the center of his brotherhood to California. The more mundane reasons, if any, for the move are not known, for Harris characteristically gave an esoteric reason, an inner light which guided him to Pacific shores for the richer revelations still to come. Furthermore, a disintegration of the "internal states" of the majority of the members at Brocton made it hard for the pivotal man properly to achieve the mental attitude necessary for revelation. Consequently, he took with him to Santa Rosa in the beginning only four of the most faithful of the brotherhood: Mrs. Requa and her son, and two Japanese, Kanaye Nagasawa and Arai. Mrs. Harris and Jane Lee Waring were soon called westward and moved with the others into the large house after its completion in November. The Brocton community remained in active existence till 1881 when all remaining members were moved to California. During the first years of the new home, however, Harris called from Brocton only those who had achieved an advanced degree of internal respiration. Brocton during that time provided an effective method of screening members for community existence, of testing individual capacities for co-operative life.

[11]*Star-Flowers* (3 vols., Fountain Grove, 1886), I, 61, 91.

[12]Arthur A. Cuthbert, *The Life and World-work of Thomas Lake Harris* (Glasgow, 1909), p. 131. Hereafter cited as Cuthbert.

So began the colony at Fountain Grove, California, "this new Eden of the West" where "the mightier Muse enkindles now."[13] The setting was indeed lovely. For $21,000 Harris had purchased over 700 acres of land sprawling over the low foothills on the sunny side of the valley about two miles above Santa Rosa. A few years later he almost doubled the acreage. At the time of the colony's founding, Santa Rosa had been linked with San Francisco by rail for five years, but the stage still ran north from Cloverdale and the local papers still reported stage robberies. Only forty-eight men of the township, including Thomas Lake Harris, had property holdings which exceeded $10,000 assessed valuation.[14]

The wine industry was already well established in Sonoma County; California growers, however, were still groping to discover the precise variety to be planted on each varying soil and hillside, and small fortunes had already been lost on mistaken hunches. Harris, surprisingly, did not at first direct the brotherhood to plant vines. Grapes had been grown at Brocton and earlier at Amenia, but for the first five years Fountain Grove was predominantly a dairy farm. By 1880, however, Edward B. Hyde and Nagasawa began the slow work of transforming the sleepy pastures and rocky slopes into vineyards. By 1884, 1,700 acres were bearing cabernet, pinot noir, and zinfandel. Two years later 70,000 gallons of wine were pressed from Fountain Grove grapes.[15]

Purely economic reasons may have dictated the late introduction of grapes at Fountain Grove. A widespread depression in the wine industry had reached its nadir in 1875. Grapes sold for eight dollars a ton and sometimes were fed to hogs. A few years later the prices had returned to around twenty-five dollars a

[13]Harris, *Star-Flowers*, III, 5.

[14]*Sonoma Democrat*, July 22, 1876. For stage robberies see *ibid.*, Jan. 28, 1882. Robert Louis Stevenson also described this area at the time as "a land of stage-drivers and highwaymen." *Silverado Squatters* (London, 1883), p. 15.

[15]Idwal Jones, *Vines in the Sun* (N.Y., 1949), pp. 22, 132, 137; *Sonoma Democrat*, Oct. 26, 1886.

ton.[16] Fountain Grove planted its vineyards as prices recovered.

Such economic and commercial considerations were, however, never the central theme of any brotherhood activities. Mystical reasons for making wine were more important than monetary considerations. Harris conceived of the spirit of fraternity and love as infusing itself from the hearts and souls of the brothers into the crushed and fermenting juices. "The wine so made and dispensed by consecrated hands devoted to human service, carried with it—and still carries—in such degree and measure as God alone knows of, like substance of Divine and celestial energy . . . to all who receive and partake of it."[17]

Nor was wine the only product to transmit the spirit of the community. Harris looked upon any object as concealing within itself the passion, the degradation, or the aspiration of the man who made it. Thus from a suit of clothes might exude all the debased desire and disease of the slum-bred tailor. From the very beginning of communal activity at Amenia and Brocton crafts were encouraged which could not possibly be economically profitable, like the community hotel and coffee shop which meted out brotherhood to the weary and hungry. The colony sought to uplift every trade by pouring into each particular commerce a small but potent catalyst infusing the spirit of freedom and joy in unselfish work.

Members of the community at Fountain Grove evidenced real consecration to their appointed tasks. Arai worked endless hours at typesetting. Hyde, when not helping Arai at the press, was devoted to his grape culture, as was Nagasawa. Alice Oliphant was indefatigable at housework. Every person served humanity while he performed his individual task, for by the theory of infusion any object would inspire its subsequent holder with the inner light of its former owner. Harris could thus proclaim that

---

[16]Robert A. Thompson, *Central Sonoma* (Santa Rosa, 1884), p. 51. See also A. Haraszthy's and E. Hilgard's statements, "The Culture of the Grape," in State of California, *Appendix to the Journals of the 23rd Sess. of the Legislature* (Sacramento, 1880), V, 7, 9.

[17]Cuthbert, p. 55 fn.

community work was a species of religious devotion. Cuthbert, one of the brothers, reflected this attitude toward labor and the consequences of its dereliction:

Being willing ourselves to serve was the one first condition . . . upon which the life could be lived. No one desiring to be idle, and not to serve with the others, could have retained the Breath for an instant without its becoming subject to furious and fatal attack from the inversive Breath of the world and of the infernal spirits of evil below the world.[18]

Harris believed that no man's work should be measured, like lumps of coal, in material productivity, but rather in the degree and extent of a man's spiritual gift to his product and through it to mankind.

This unusual spiritual devotion to labor was responsible in part for the special name the brotherhood gave to the community. "Our community here we often call 'The Use'. Everyone . . . must have his or her 'use' or 'uses', according to his or her special genius."[19] Harris had undoubtedly adapted the word from Swedenborg, who had written: "To perform use is to will well to others for the sake of the common good; but to will well to others not for the sake of the common good but for the sake of self is not to perform use."[20]

The individual's devotion to the task at hand was not the result of a free choice of occupations within the Use. Although for purely practical reasons Harris did not stretch the man too far from his desired or fitting position, yet Harris remained the arbiter.

He will select tillers of the soil, and they will till the vast domain. He will select artists and artisans, and they will build the Bridal City. These workers will fit into the purpose of the king even as the sword fits into the scabbard; and in this unity of the social-will the dreamed-of paradise will rise on earth.[21]

[18]Cuthbert, p. 49.

[19]Margaret O. W. Oliphant, *Memoir of the Life of Laurence Oliphant* (2 vols., N.Y., 1891), II, 40; hereafter cited as Oliphant, *Memoir*.

[20]Swedenborg, *Heaven and Hell* (N.Y., 1938), p. 34.

[21]Harris, "Glimpses of Social and Sexual Order" (unpub. MS, n.d., Columbia University Library), p. 2.

The physical backdrop for this work consisted of six buildings set into niches in the foothills. The colony road wound up a quarter of a mile from the highway and leveled just before reaching the first group of buildings. On the left in the trees stood the lovely and imposing Harris home, named by Harris "Aestivossa," with two stories and a spacious attic, a wide entrance porch on the north, and sun-rooms spreading from the first story to the south. Inside, the rooms were high-ceilinged and paneled, with thick Oriental carpets and stained-glass windows depicting angels and knights. Several sitting-rooms, the library, an immense dining room, and a kitchen filled the lower story, with bedrooms and smaller rooms overhead. Gas pumped from gasoline lit the whole house, the washrooms had marble stands, and the water-closets were all connected with the house, making, in a contemporary description, "a little palace within itself."[22] In this mansion lived Harris, his wife, Emily, Jane Lee Waring, Alice Oliphant, and a few others of a similarly select station. The remaining members of the community resided in a large familistère, standing directly across the road from the house, composed of two stories and constructed of paneled and polished redwood. Nearby was a small house of hasty construction built to shelter Harris and his group during the summer of 1875 while the larger house was rising. About thirty people dwelt in these three central buildings.

The winery, the brandy house, and their necessary outbuildings stood another quarter-mile up the road in the midst of the vineyards. Some years later the brotherhood built a round barn with a conical roof. Except for the great familistère which was burned in the early twentieth century, all of the buildings still stand.

Harris could create an impressive and costly establishment because he was blessed with wealthy followers. Laurence Oliphant, according to his cousin, assigned all his fortune to the community, as did his bride-to-be, Alice le Strange. When Oliphant seceded

[22]Santa Rosa *Daily Democrat*, Nov. 23, 1875.

from the colony, Harris settled his claims for restitution with a reputed $90,000, suggesting the extent to which the Oliphants helped fill the communal coffers. Many entering members, like the Partings, turned over ample worldly belongings to Harris, and sizable donations likewise flowed from non-resident sympathizers like the Ruxton family in England.[23]

Around the main house at Fountain Grove, gardens and lawns and hedged ponds instilled the feeling of repose and retreat. Harris consciously tried to induce such a temper in his followers. "It is by probing the mystery of Solitude . . . that the seeker finds, in the end, the path into the spirit of Society. . . . I am but the servant of the Solitude. . . ."[24] And in case the Fountain Grove asylum was invaded by treacherous fays or the spirits of evil, Harris provided himself with an additional retreat in the mountains eight miles to the south and named this rustic cabin Linn Lilla.

The feeling of solitude at Fountain Grove, however, did not imply a monastic life. Members ate together in the large communal dining hall, sometimes singing, always joining hands around the table for grace. For many months Harris enlivened breakfast by providing a new poem each morning, light verse personifying sprightly characters from the fay world.[25] The year 1886 ushered in a particularly gay period for Fountain Grove, when Harris conceived of important spiritual vitalities as flowing through his people by means of music and the dance. "You would smile to see the full sisterhood, all in beautiful attire, and gliding through quadrilles as if they had wings on their feet, while the brethren old and young, look on and wonder and smile and dance with

[23]Oliphant, *Memoir*, II, 30, 115. The $90,000 figure is repeated in the San Francisco *Chronicle*, Feb. 10, 1885, and June 21, 1891, by two separate investigating reporters. In the absence of more reliable sources, the figure is used here as a general indication only. The San Francisco *Chronicle*, Feb. 10, 1885, reported the case of T. J. Miller who sold his ranch in San Bernardino and turned over the $3,000 to Harris when he joined the colony in 1879.

[24]Harris, "A Letter to a Seeker in Retreat" (unpub. MS, Columbia University Library).

[25]Later collected as *The Golden Child; A Daily Chronicle*, Part I, *Songs of Fairyland* (n.p., 1878).

them till the house quivers."[26] But even such apparently frivolous gaiety had a veiled purpose.

> If you would slay the Social Snake,
> That brings the bosom grief and ache,
> Dance while you may, dance while you may,
> For Heaven comes forth in social play.[27]

Communal singing was popular, especially hymns of the New Life, such as "With Roses Wreathe the Drum," "Social Resurrection," and "Arrows of the Sun." Words and music were reproduced and distributed until the songs were learned. The main house contained a carefully tuned piano at which Harris, without any previous musical training, could play and thereby invoke his Lily Queen into "electro-vital form."[28]

The problem of sex relationships within the community at Fountain Grove is complicated by the cabalistic nature of the doctrines and by the publication of misunderstandings in the outside world. Harris' own life, however, provides some help in explanation. His mother, Annie Lake Harris, died when the boy was only nine, and the unhappy home created by his stepmother resulted in an idolization of his own mother. In 1878 he recorded how the sight of a little child could recall in him his mother's image,[29] and as late as 1886 he dedicated *Star-Flowers* to her in flowing verses. Harris himself had three successive wives. He married first when he was twenty-two and his first wife bore him two sons in a five-year period. These were his only children and the death of their mother in 1850 contributed to Harris' deep involvement in spiritualism at that time. He married his second wife, Emily, in 1855, both husband and wife maintaining that the thirty-year marriage which followed was absolutely celibate.

[26]Letter from Harris, April 14, 1886, in Schneider, p. 443. See also Cuthbert, pp. 354-55.

[27]Harris, "The Joy-Bringer," in Cuthbert, pp. 350-51.

[28]Cuthbert, p. 217.

[29]*The Golden Child: A Daily Chronicle*, Part IV, p. 5.

The third marriage to Jane Lee Waring, seven years after "Emmie's" death, was also assertedly purely platonic. Harris' own published and unpublished statements regarding marital relations are perfectly proper and decorous. Indeed, as we have seen, he repudiated Andrew Jackson Davis because of the latter's immoral relations with a married woman. Harris' desire for celibacy was partly based upon his abhorrence of the laxity of external society in sex ethics. "Humankind has become so diseased and disordered that they can come into a period of health and order only by a period of complete separation between the sexes."[30]

These ideas and statements, however, were not sufficient to guard the community against allegations of scandal, deduced from misunderstandings of Harris' religious doctrines. Harris proclaimed a bisexual diety, a "Twain-One Lord," based upon his own revelation and upon Genesis. If God created man in his own image and "male and female created He them," then God must be Himself both male and female. God becomes one with Himself and man comes closest to being one with God when the sexes are united spiritually. In one of Harris' first revelations, an angel had commanded him:

Sing of love, dear brother . . . sing of conjugial love. Be the poet of Maidens and Lovers, and Conjugial Consorts. Make thy poetic house a garden of Eden where the Adams and Eves of the Golden Age shall sing their endless marriage-hymn.[31]

Heaven became a Bridal Palace with all the carnal states of sexuality swept away.

In a theory which combined spiritualism with his own sex ideas, Harris disclosed that the true spiritual union of the sexes was consummated in a "counterpart." The counterpart, which existed in heaven but was able temporarily to inhabit earthly human forms, could be reached only in a state of mind achieved

[30]Harris, "Heart Wants of London" (unpub. MS, n.d., Columbia University Library).

[31]Harris, The Wisdom of Angels (N.Y., 1857), p. 155.

through the Divine Breath and would only in exceptional cases coincide with the spirit of one's earthly spouse. The union of the counterparts became a mystical experience in which "every man and woman is married to very God. God Himself is the only real Bridegroom, God Herself is the only real Bride."[32]

Harris often referred to the California colony in phrases which invited misunderstanding from outsiders.

> Here shall Hymen have his court,
> And every priest a Cupid be,
> Till golden babes are born to sport,
> Where lift the waves of Mother-Glee,
> Borne through this vast Pacific Sea.[33]

The actual applications of the theories provided grounds for further misunderstanding. Harris occasionally interfered drastically with the normal pattern of family life. Any relationship which broke the flow of communal harmony was immediately discontinued. Thus parents on occasion were separated from children and husbands from wives. Harris justified such breaches as preparation for the divine marriage, as means to stay earthly lusts, or as attempts to block excessive love for an individual in order to encourage the wider flow of love for mankind.

Laurence Oliphant, his mother, and his wife furnished the most noteworthy example of Harris' interference in family life. When Oliphant abandoned his seat in the British Parliament and repaired to the Harris colony at Amenia, he had been a bachelor, closely drawn to his mother, Lady Oliphant, who had preceded him in joining the New York group. For months Harris separated the mother from the son, never permitting them to meet or talk, basing his action on Oliphant's need for undisturbed preparation for the New Life. Harris secluded Oliphant in the lonely loft of a barn and allowed him not even a glimpse of his mother for months at a time. Some years later, when the community sent Oliphant as its representative to Europe, he met Miss Alice le Strange in

[32]Cuthbert, p. 157.

[33]Harris, *Star-Flowers*, III, 6.

Paris and was immediately captivated. Laurence, however, would not marry without the blessing of his spiritual father, and Harris required Alice to offer complete fealty and faith before permitting the marriage. When the two returned to the community, a normal married life, even on the level of companionship, was never granted them. Throughout their years with the brotherhood they lived separately, seldom seeing one another. Harris took Alice with him to California while directing Laurence to continue his work in New York. This strained relationship between two people who gave every indication of being deeply in love paved the way for a dramatic rupture between Oliphant and Harris in 1881.

Oliphant's isolation from his mother and wife was, of course, the separation of adults. But children were likewise segregated from parents when Harris believed the spiritual needs of each so indicated. The Cuthbert and Requa children were not housed with their own families because of the inferior mental states of the parents at the time of conception and birth. Harris felt that these offspring were particularly susceptible to evil spirits and therefore should receive the special care and protection of the entire community. The colony considered the separated children especially lucky because they had not one mother but many.

As far as is known, no illegitimate and very few legitimate children were ever born into the Harris colonies. In 1877 Harris admitted, "One young pair in our borders have had three children, I am sorry to say; but with this exception the births in seventeen years [i.e., including the Brocton period] have been but two. . . ."[34] Harris occasionally permitted marriage when he felt the individuals concerned were not sufficiently advanced spiritually to remain celibate. These marriages were founded on the usual civil contract. When he himself married Jane Lee Waring in 1892, the ceremony was performed by an Episcopalian clergyman and duly recorded by the civil authorities.

A question almost as clouded as that of sex relationships is the

---

[34]In letter to W. A. Hinds, Fountain Grove, Aug. 22, 1877, in Hinds, *American Communities* (Oneida, N.Y., 1878), p. 146.

degree to which Fountain Grove property could be called communal. Legally all ownership rested in the name of Harris, but theoretically he only held in trust worldly possessions belonging to the community as a whole. As for the disposition of personal property at the time of admission, there were no set rules, no constitutions or by-laws, and each case was an ordinance unto itself. Harris once said that "there is here no 'community'; every friend controls his own property and manages his own affairs. Some of the brothers carry on business on their individual account; others in co-operation or partnership."[35] And Cuthbert wrote, "There never was ... community of possessions in The Use, in any legal sense. Every individual was duly invested with his own share of all properties, corresponding to his means, but of course all were essentially involved together in their increasing or lowering market values."[36] In these statements the community appears as one in which economic equality was unimportant if not nonexistent. On the other hand, Harris constantly preached against the possession of private property for individual ends, and many members gave up all their assets to Harris when joining the colony.

When Laurence Oliphant attached himself to the community, as we have already seen, he relinquished all of his worldly possessions. The same was true of his wife, Alice, when she became a member. Theoretically when anyone was admitted, he surrendered all his property to the common fund; but in practice no clear rule prevailed. Rumors that Harris in California was pressing Brocton members to release and convey their remaining private holdings indicated that at least some personal property existed. After the split in 1881, Oliphant recovered much of his investment, and this eventual dispensation hints that the original gift was not an outright surrender of property. On the other hand, few members ever recovered their donations as did Oliphant. The community was never as loose an arrangement as Oliphant once described it: "So far as property goes, we are neighbors and

---

[35]Letter from Harris, Feb. 8, 1871, in Oliphant, *Memoir*, II, 132.
[36]Cuthbert, p. 191.

nothing more."[37] Some members of the colony, especially those
with few or small property holdings, transmitted all they possessed when entering the brotherhood; others, like the Oliphants
and the Partings, maintained large degrees of control over their
own affairs and gave to the community only periodic donations.

Harris' own ideas on private property are no more clear-cut
than the practices of the community. He shuddered at the misuse
of private property: "The possession of property held for individual ends, grapples man and fixes him in a selfish and fatal
individualism and isolation from his fellows . . . ,"[38] and again that
the transfer of private property into public property . . . was commanded by the Lord Jesus." But he repudiated communism because it denied both personal liberty and his own revealed religion.

I could not live at Lebanon [the Shakers], I could not breathe at
Oneida. . . . For Owenism, notwithstanding the merits of its distinguished founder, I also entertain only a partial sympathy. . . . I recognize an immense truth and good in many of the features of these
working communities . . . [but] as the world goes, we are not communists; we follow neither the celibate idea, nor the perfectionist
ideal, nor the red republic banner. I recognize no right in the natural
man to share my goods . . . ; and by the natural man I mean any man
whose natural passion is the rule of self."

Harris was a religious equalitarian and refused a materialistic
communism. The property which he administered for the community became in his eyes a spiritual realm, and the extent of
individual secular holdings was secondary as long as the brethren
shared the fundamental unity of religious belief.

Harris preferred to call his community, not communism, but
Theo-Socialism. This particular brand of socialism had its roots
in Harris' early humanitarianism and his divination of the Social
Gospel. The slum conditions of London and Manchester had

[37] This statement, in a letter to Laurence's brother-in-law, was undoubtedly
meant to allay fears concerning Alice's property; Oliphant, *Memoir*, II, 30, 115,
120, 207-208; Schneider, pp. 162, 339.

[38] Harris, "Private Property and Social Life in the Light of the Christ" (unpub.
MS, n.d., Columbia University Library), p. 1. The following two quotes are from
ibid., pp. 2, 15.

distressed him as a young Swedenborgian minister in 1859 and 1860. Later he inspired Horace Greeley to found the New York Juvenile Asylum.[39] In the *New Republic* he spoke of the Social Christ, the "Socialist of socialists." Harris' use of the term was courageous in an era when socialists were so widely derided and when Americans as a whole scornfully lumped under that epithet every form of discontent from tax reform to anarchism. Perhaps for this reason, Harris maintained that his Theo-Socialism was unlike any other type of socialism.

All men free and equal by reason of the Divine immanence within them! Add to this, all men fraternal by virtue of the Divine Father-Motherhood, educing the divine-human sonship and daughterhood throughout the free, coequal, interdependent all;—then we have ... the creed of the Social Christ. ..."[40]

Harris made this statement in 1891 when he was deeply concerned with worldly politics and external affairs. He attended labor meetings and wrote songs which were sung at labor gatherings. He followed the course of Edward Bellamy's Nationalist Clubs with eager interest. All during 1891 he poured forth the themes of socialism, industrialism, and government in a long succession of pamphlets and books, all dealing with political and social subjects.

Harris found external socialism in error because it was not based on religion. Furthermore, he would have had socialists adopt some of the methods of monopolistic capitalism. Small co-operative communities should provide the base for an expanding hierarchy of co-operative units, just as industrial divisions were linked into giant monopolies. In this picture he clearly reflected Bellamy's Nationalism. Rather than Bellamy, however, Harris found Laurence Gronlund, American author of the *Co-operative Commonwealth*, the most penetrating social thinker of the time. Gronlund's fundamental Marxism provided Harris with a satisfactory analysis of the industrial and economic laws, but Gronlund had gone beyond Marx by minimizing the class struggle and emphasizing

[39]Cuthbert, pp. 109-110; Harris, *New Republic* (Santa Rosa, 1891), pp. 67-68.
[40]Harris, *New Republic*, p. 23.

the growth of man's ability to co-operate. Gronlund was a far cry from a Harrisite Theo-Socialist, but for Harris he pointed more satisfactorily toward the goal of Theo-Socialism than did any other utopian or Marxian socialist.

Inevitably in an alien culture and increasingly as the years progressed, misunderstandings of the community's theology and communism developed. In the 1870's and early 1880's the local newspapers and the local and county histories pictured Harris as no more than an English squire presiding over a landscaped country estate. The sketch was sometimes modified to that of a wealthy New Yorker creating a retreat for winter vacations and the entertainment of eastern friends. His library was described as the most extensive in California, while his theology was briefly dispatched as a harmless quirk. Most of these early pictures made Harris a highly respectable and conventional man. They never came closer to his colony ideas than to mention his vast properties in New York state and his founding of the First National Bank at Amenia. Fountain Grove, it would seem, was no more related to socialism than any baronial plantation.[41]

Around 1891 the picture was reversed and troubles began to multiply for both Harris and the community. The storm broke with the publication of Margaret Oliphant's biography of her cousin Laurence.[42] The book eulogized the late Laurence and his wife, but accused Harris by implication of immorality and financial chicanery. Before the newspapers exploited this sensational story, a more startling one appeared. Miss Alzire A. Chevaillier, a professional agitator, Christian Scientist, Nationalist, and suffragette, and her mother had arrived as visitors at Fountain Grove in the summer of 1891. A few months later they left indignantly, having taken umbrage at supposed advances of the primate toward

---

[41]Santa Rosa *Daily Democrat*, Nov. 23, 1875. J. P. Munro-Frazer, *History of Sonoma County* (San Francisco, 1879), pp. 428-29. *An Illustrated History of Sonoma County, Calif.* (Chicago, 1889), p. 367. One hostile article, however, foreshadowing later developments, appeared in the San Francisco *Chronicle*, Feb. 10, 1885.

[42]Margaret O. W. Oliphant, *Memoir of the Life of Laurence Oliphant* (2 vols., N.Y., 1891).

Miss Chevaillier. Most of the Chevaillier accusations, which immediately began appearing in the press, concerned the autocracy of
Harris and the slavery of his members, a state which the brothers
themselves welcomed as true freedom. The suggestions of sexual
license and immorality were all admittedly based on hearsay
or innuendo.

The statements, however, received widespread publicity. The
story of a pretended celibate monk luring innocent maidens to
his den in the mountains flamed in all the Santa Rosa and San
Francisco newspapers. Miss Chevaillier lectured in Santa Rosa to
packed halls. Wild stories arose such as a reference to the poisoning
of Harris' non-existent daughter.[43] Harris personally made few
public denials or countercharges; he professed "no more than a
kindly contempt" for the press, prowling about the "kitchen
middens . . . [with] the smell of the waste-pipes."[44] Events were
simply fulfilling the prophecy and the warning he had given to
his brotherhood:

> Come unto me, My People, come and share
> Denial, shame, fierce wrath, and condemnation.[45]

Harris nevertheless must have felt the external hostility more
deeply than he wished to say. He was aware of the difficulty or
impossibility of correcting errors once they are lodged in the
public consciousness. Since most of the Oliphant and Chevaillier
charges had been aimed at him and had absolved the members of
the community as mere victims of his wiles, Harris considered
it best to abandon Fountain Grove. But before leaving, in one

[43]The first notice of Chevaillier at Fountain Grove appeared in the San Fran-
cisco *Chronicle*, June 11, 1891. Her sensational charges began in the *Chronicle*,
Dec. 13 and 27, 1891, and Feb. 15, 1892. They were picked up by other San Fran-
cisco papers: The *Wave*, Feb. 13, 1892, and the *Morning Call*, Mar. 4, 1892. As for
the Santa Rosa papers, the controversy appeared in the *Sonoma Democrat*,
Jan. 30, Feb. 20, and Feb. 27, 1892, and in the *Daily Republican*, Feb. 22, 1892.
See also Frank Bailey Millard, *History of the San Francisco Bay Region* (3 vols.,
Chicago, 1924), I, 459-64; and, for the rumor regarding Harris' daughter, Idwal
Jones, *Vines in the Sun*, p. 139.

[44]Harris, *Brotherhood of the New Life* (Fountain Grove, 1891), p. 12.

[45]Harris, in Cuthbert, ff. p. 413.

last defiant gesture, on February 27, 1892, he married Jane Lee
Waring who had served him for over thirty years and for at least
seventeen years had been his chief secretary and assistant. Harris'
second wife had long been dead, but the marriage with Jane Lee
Waring produced a howl from the press. "No More a Celibate,"
headlined the San Francisco *Call* on March 4, 1892, and the *Chronicle* on the same day carried a front-page story about the "wedded
mystics."

The groom of sixty-eight years with his bride of sixty-four
departed for Europe and nevermore returned to Fountain Grove.
They later took up residence in a New York apartment which
they christened "the Gateway of the Comfortings." The money
Harris received from his Fountain Grove interest carried him
and his wife comfortably through their remaining years, including winters in Florida and summers in New Brunswick. He died
in 1906 at the age of eighty-three.

Fountain Grove became, after Harris' departure, progressively
less a communitarian experiment and more a commercial venture.
For some years Harris tried to control the group by arbitrary
decisions from New York, but with results more confusing than
effective. Without the personality of Harris to hold them, the
members gradually drifted away. Harris' presence was, after all,
the principle *raison d'être* for their communal existence. In 1900
Harris sold all of his remaining claim for $40,000 to five members
of the colony. A clause in the deed provided that the property
should revert to the one who lived longest and to his heirs and
assigns. Thus Kanaye Nagasawa became the sole owner in the
1920's and managed the Fountain Grove Winery till his death in
1934. Thereafter the property passed into the hands of outsiders
and only a few scattered members of the brotherhood remembered
its former consecration. Harris' inspired dream "of the New
Harmonic Civilization; of the ending of all feuds, the vanishment
of all diseases, the abolishment of all antagonisms,"[46] had foundered, like the New York colony of Oneida, in the publicized
misunderstandings of an esoteric sexual theory.

[46]Harris, *Brotherhood of the New Life*, p. 1.

CHAPTER 3

Theosophical Colonies in California: Point Loma and Temple Home

IVE years after Thomas Lake Harris departed from Fountain Grove, on a February afternoon in 1897 nearly a thousand residents of San Diego ascended the bluff, where Point Loma juts into the sea, to witness a momentous Theosophical ceremony. In a purple gown with embroidered emblems, Katherine Augusta Westcott Tingley sprinkled corn and oil and wine on a cornerstone surrounded by ropes of cypress. Colorful banners caught the sunlight. Flags waved from the derrick which held the stone. A band from San Diego softly played Mascagni's "Intermezzo" as Mrs. Tingley, the central figure of the ceremonies, lowered a metal box into the rock, smoothed the mortar with a silver trowel, and proclaimed, "I dedicate this stone; a perfect square, a fitting emblem of the perfect work that will be done in the temple for the benefit of humanity and glory of the ancient sages."[1] Katherine Tingley's words, juxtaposing humanitarianism with occult wisdom, sounded a keynote which would ring over the Universal Brotherhood and Theosophical Society at Point Loma for half a century to come.

The ceremony stretched through the afternoon. A dozen speeches followed readings from the Bhagavad-Gita, the Upanishads and the Orphic Mysteries. But the San Diegans remained, often in hushed awe, curious to know more of this settlement

---

[1]San Diego *Union* and San Francisco *Chronicle*, Feb. 24, 1897.

about to rise at their front gate. Mrs. Tingley's announcements had foretold the International Headquarters of a Universal Brotherhood, splendid communal buildings, a school and a college, and a world center for the arts and sciences.

Katherine Tingley was at this time just emerging as a leader of the Theosophical world, a vigorous woman with a stout frame, dark hair, and grey, restless eyes.[2] She had been born in Newburyport, Massachusetts, in 1852, but much of her early life was spent with her grandfather in woodlands along the Merrimac River. She married three times but had no children of her own. While living in New York City with her last husband, Philo B. Tingley, an inventor, her first philanthropic interests blossomed. In 1887 she established the Society of Mercy; two years later, the Martha Washington Home for the Aged; two years after that, the Do-Good Mission for emergency relief on the East Side of New York. From that time her life might be summarized as one extensive humanitarian venture. She organized, directly or indirectly, a children's home on the Palisades of the Hudson and another in Buffalo, the Sisters of Compassion to aid wounded soldiers from the Spanish-American War, relief expeditions to Cuba, and, at Point Loma, a series of humanitarian crusades ranging from the education of foreign children and the promotion of world peace to the abolition of vivisection and capital punishment. At the time of her early philanthropies, she became interested in spiritualism and, during the nineties, took the final step into Theosophy. William Quan Judge, the leading Theosophist in America, not only converted her, but helped her rise rapidly in Theosophical circles. Before his death in 1896, he designated her his successor as Outer Head of the Theosophical Society.

The society had by this time celebrated its twentieth birthday. Its founder and patron-saint, Helena Petrovna Blavatsky, was born in southern Russia in 1831, a "reckless, self-willed, erratic"

[2]Ray Stannard Baker, "An Extraordinary Experiment in Brotherhood," *American Magazine*, LXIII (Jan., 1907), 236. Biographical details also in Katherine Tingley, *The Gods Await* (Point Loma, Calif., 1926), pp. 75-80.

child.[3] When still in her teens, she married a seventy-year-old general, Nicephore Blavatsky, but promptly abandoned him and spent the next ten years drifting through the capitals of Europe. In Paris, in 1858, she embraced spiritualism, and by the time she arrived in New York in 1873 she had developed spiritualistic powers which were regarded as miraculous.

At various occult gatherings in and around New York Madame Blavatsky met Henry Steel Olcott, a lawyer who was at the time writing a series of articles on spiritualism for the New York *Daily Graphic*. The two spiritualists became devoted friends, and on September 7, 1875, they formed a group for the study of the occult which became the Theosophical Society.

During the early years while the society grew slowly, Madame Blavatsky produced the two lengthy volumes of *Isis Unveiled*. Herein she announced her break with spiritualism, as had Thomas Lake Harris before her, and hazily sketched the basic principles of the Theosophical Society, principles she later elaborated in *The Secret Doctrine*. True spiritualism, she maintained, should be a "culture of the spirits of the living, not a commerce with the souls of the dead."[4]

In December, 1878, Madame Blavatsky and Olcott, in order to enlarge the scope of their new society, sailed for India by way of England. Leaving William Quan Judge, their most trusted lieutenant, in control in America, they now initiated branches in the British Isles and the Orient. In 1879 they established the International Headquarters of the Theosophical Society, first at Bombay and shortly thereafter at Adyar, a suburb of Madras, and here Olcott remained for the rest of his life. Following 1880 the organization mushroomed until at the time of Olcott's death in 1907 over six hundred branches met in forty-two different countries; during the late 1890's Theosophists gathered in over

[3]Ernest Sutherland Bates, "Helena Petrovna Blavatsky," *DAB*. For more extensive treatments of Blavatsky's life, see Charles J. Ryan, *H. P. Blavatsky and the Theosophical Movement* (Point Loma, 1937); Alvin B. Kuhn, *Theosophy* (N.Y., 1930); Gertrude M. Williams, *Priestess of the Occult* (N.Y., 1946).

[4]In Alvin Kuhn, *Theosophy*, p. 96.

a hundred chapters in the United States alone, California claiming more lodges than any other state.[5]

Madame Blavatsky held the post of Corresponding Secretary of the society, but she was far more than a mere administrator. She received letters of guidance from the Mahatmas, the Great White Brotherhood of men, living in the Himalayas, who through successive reincarnations, it was claimed, had achieved super-human levels of wisdom. Madame Blavatsky dominated the order as the pivotal link between the Mahatmas and the membership at large. In the 1880's one of her secretaries and the London Society for Psychical Research charged forgery of the alleged letters from the Mahatmas, thereby deeply stirring Theosophical waters and causing Madame Blavatsky's immediate return to England. In the face of popular indignation, she officially withdrew as Corresponding Secretary of the society but within a few years appeared again in London as leader of a new branch, to be known as the Esoteric Section.

During this stay in London, Madame Blavatsky attracted to the society Annie Besant, who was speedily to become one of its most remarkable leaders. Mrs. Besant, like Mrs. Tingley, was deep-rooted in humanitarianism. Her life had been marked by several distinct phases: after a religious youth and marriage to an orthodox Anglican clergyman she had become an atheist, freethinker, and crusader for birth control and free speech; and, still later, socialist and leading member of the Fabian Society. In 1889 she shocked George Bernard Shaw and her other Fabian associates by proclaiming her conversion to Theosophy. She had read *The Secret Doctrine* in order to review it and, deeply impressed, had immediately sought the author, exposing herself fully to the dynamic magnetism of Madame Blavatsky's personality. To the world Mrs. Besant stated simply that Theosophy answered the questions she had been asking for the greater part of her life. Following her conversion, Annie Besant rose quickly

[5]H. S. Olcott, "Theosophy and Theosophists," *Overland Monthly* (San Francisco), XXXVII (May, 1901), 995, 997; Kuhn, *Theosophy*, Chap. XII; E. S. Bates, "Henry Steel Olcott," *DAB*.

THEOSOPHICAL SOCIETIES IN AMERICA

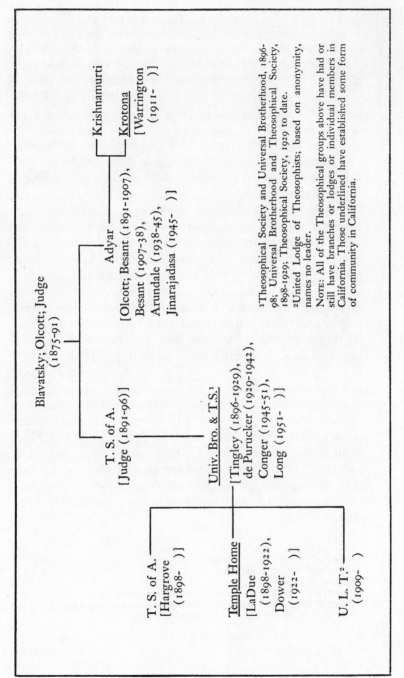

Blavatsky; Olcott; Judge
(1875-91)

Adyar —
[Olcott; Besant (1891-1907),
Besant (1907-38),
Arundale (1938-45),
Jinarajadasa (1945-)]

Krishnamurti

Krotona
[Warrington
(1911-)]

T. S. of A.
[Judge (1891-96)]

Univ. Bro. & T.S.[1]
[Tingley (1896-1929),
de Purucker (1929-1942),
Conger (1945-51),
Long (1951-)]

T. S. of A.
[Hargrove
(1898-)]

Temple Home
[LaDue
(1898-1922),
Dower
(1922-)]

U. L. T.[2]
(1909-)

[1]Theosophical Society and Universal Brotherhood, 1896-98; Universal Brotherhood and Theosophical Society, 1898-1929; Theosophical Society, 1929 to date.

[2]United Lodge of Theosophists; based on anonymity, names no leader.

NOTE: All of the Theosophical groups above have had or still have branches or lodges or individual members in California. Those underlined have established some form of community in California.

to prominence in the society, her home became Madame Blavatsky's headquarters, and after Madame Blavatsky's death in 1891, she inherited the leadership of the Adyar branch.[6]

As a system of thought, theosophy antedated Madame Blavatsky by centuries. The word itself suggests "divine wisdom," and has often been used to designate a philosophy based on mystical insight into a Divine Nature. In this sense Meister Eckhardt in the fourteenth century, Jakob Boehme in the seventeenth, Emanuel Swedenborg in the eighteenth, and Friedrich von Schelling in the nineteenth, all exemplified theosophical thought. Madame Blavatsky, however, rendered the generalized philosophy into a more systematic, abstruse doctrine. Her basic postulate, with which all earlier theosophists would have agreed, pictured the universe centered, not in a personal God, but in a boundless, omnipresent, eternal Principle. Her second premise, at which earlier theosophists would have begun to frown, revealed a creation moving in cyclical patterns with innumerable universes emerging and disappearing within the totality of the encompassing Principle. Her third basic idea, reminiscent of Emerson, identified all souls with the universal Soul, proclaiming a unity of all life, indeed, of all creation. Every soul, however, struggled in an upward pilgrimage; thus within the unity of life ranged a hierarchy based upon the degree of nearness to the universal Soul.

These Blavatskian doctrines can be more concretely understood in their final embodiment as the principles of the Theosophical Society. Like all things theosophical, the objectives of the society evolved noticeably from 1875 to 1891, but by 1882 they had assumed intrinsically the form in which they have remained, with varying emphases, to the present day. These objectives were:

---

[6]The great schism over succession following Blavatsky's death left the society split with William Quan Judge in control in America and Annie Besant with Henry Steel Olcott ruling from the East. Both sections continued to claim international followings, and local lodges were forced to choose between the two factions. Judge lived thereafter for only five years, and when he died in 1896, Katherine Tingley succeeded him without, however, uniting Eastern sections to the Western. Besant and Tingley were never congenial.

1—To form the nucleus of a Universal Brotherhood of Humanity without distinction of race, creed, sex, caste, or color.

2—To promote the study of Aryan and other Eastern literature, religions, and sciences.

3—To investigate the hidden mysteries of Nature and the psychical powers latent in man.

The brotherhood aim grew to overshadow the original purpose, the study of the occult. By Katherine Tingley's time, and especially under her leadership, brotherhood became a foundation for all the other objectives. Elements within the society constantly resisted the tendency away from psychic investigations, but Katherine Tingley led her own branch into such an emphasis on brotherhood that she even insisted on the society's name being changed to "The Universal Brotherhood and Theosophical Society."

The idea of brotherhood flowed logically from the Blavatskian unity of all souls and stood closely akin to a Buddhistic unity of all life.

A Brotherhood of man exists by virtue of the one life which developes in all alike. There is no stone in the road, there is no plant growing out of the earth, there is no animal that breathes the breath of life, there is no human being in whom intelligence is developed, that is not rooted in the One Life....[7]

This same belief fostered the humanitarian emphasis of the society. Theosophists considered that any action which wronged one man injured at the same time the whole of humanity. Such teachings would appear exceedingly attractive to humanitarians like Katherine Tingley and Annie Besant. Mrs. Besant's work in India, including education and campaigns to raise the position of women and to abolish child marriage, reflected as deep a humanitarian concern as had her pre-Theosophical activities based on more secular reasoning.

[7] Annie Besant, *Theosophy and the Theosophical Society* (Adyar, Madras, India, 1913), p. 84.

Further evidence of the interrelations of Theosophy and social reform emerged in the early 1890's in connection with Edward Bellamy's *Looking Backward*. The Bostonian founders of the first Nationalist Club, Cyrus Field Willard and Sylvester Baxter, were both Theosophists. Of the committee of seven appointed to draft a statement of principles, all except Bellamy himself were Theosophists.[8] The articles charted by this committee clearly reflected Theosophical ideas:

The principle of the Brotherhood of Humanity is one of the eternal truths that govern the world's progress on lines which distinguish human nature from brute nature.[9]

The founder of Theosophy herself urged extension of the relationship and in 1889 suggested that Theosophists join in efforts to realize the Nationalist ideals.[10] In California, an active center of both Nationalism and Theosophy during the early 1890's, Theosophists eagerly responded to the suggestion and instituted Nationalist clubs throughout the state.[11]

The Theosophical support of Nationalism, however, was short-lived, and the inherent conflict between the political approach of Bellamy and the more mystical leaning of his Theosophical followers erupted in 1891. The old question of reform through the individual versus reform through the environment came to a head both between the two organizations and within the Theosophical Society itself. Following Madame Blavatsky's death, the new leadership withdrew Theosophical support from the Nationalist movement, and not until the establishment of Katherine Tingley's headship did the society again commit itself to social reform.

[8] Arthur E. Morgan, *Edward Bellamy* (N.Y., 1944), p. 261.

[9] *Nationalist* (Boston), I (May, 1889), 13.

[10] *Key to Theosophy* (London and N.Y., 1889), pp. 44-45.

[11] Abbott G. Clark, Theosophical leader in California during the 1890's and later one of the chief horticulturists at Point Loma, in letter to Arthur E. Morgan, in Morgan, *Edward Bellamy*, pp. 266-67, 268-69. Vernon L. Parrington, Jr., *American Dreams* (Providence, R.I., 1947), p. 161, refers to the Theosophist Society of Oakland as an active disseminator of Bellamy's ideas in the 1890's.

The second objective of the society, the promotion of the study of Eastern literature and religion, merely expanded the first plank of brotherhood, especially in Katherine Tingley's mind. If all men were to be brothers, they should understand one another's beliefs and philosophies. Men should know that all religions stemmed from a few essentials, that the various creeds actually added to a single whole. The unity of God, divine revelation, immortality, the moral law of ethical conduct, these were the elements which Theosophists identified in all religions, using Eastern as well as Western sources for a deeper understanding of the common denominators. The great teachers of mankind—Buddha, Krishna, Confucius, Jesus—were divine, just as all men were divine. The wisdom of these spiritual masters, however, reached supernal heights and revealed an additional dimension, a deeper understanding of Truth, and no such insight, from whatever corner of the world, should be overlooked.

As for the third object of the society, the study of the occult, Madame Blavatsky herself had renounced spiritualism as ethically sterile and devoid of a philosophy to explain its manifestations. Mrs. Tingley did not deny the existence of psychical phenomena, but she minimized their importance in the present stage of human evolution and cautioned her members at Point Loma to avoid their dangers. In drafting the constitution for the Universal Brotherhood she carefully relegated the investigation of the "laws of nature and the divine powers in man" to a position subsidiary to the principle purpose of brotherhood.[12]

Theosophy's basic premises went deeper than brotherhood, comparative religion, and study of the occult. Among the theological tenets, probably the doctrines of Karma and Reincarnation attracted the greatest number of converts. In these theories the humanitarian, faced with the abyssal distress of society, found a solution to the problem of evil which was for some persons more satisfying than the traditional Christian hypothesis. If the

[12]"Constitution of the Universal Brotherhood," Archives of the Theosophical Society, Pasadena, Calif. See also Katherine Tingley, *Life at Point Loma* (Point Loma, 1908), p. 19; and *The Wine of Life* (Point Loma, 1925), pp. 181-98.

Eternal Principle or God were all-good and all-powerful, why did He allow evil in the world? The Theosophist answered that the responsibility lay not with God, or even Adam, that evil was the immediate consequence of an individual's actions in a previous incarnation. Karma represented the necessity of the individual to pay for his misdeeds; Reincarnation, the mechanism through which he made compensation and thereby rose to ultimate perfection.

The laying of the cornerstone at Point Loma in 1897 marked only one event in a World Theosophical Crusade, Katherine Tingley's first official move after her accession to leadership in 1896. She, with five prominent Theosophists, had circled the globe, lecturing and founding local lodges. During this lengthy tour, she formulated plans for the Universal Brotherhood and school. While still in Europe she arranged for the purchase of land on Point Loma and at every opportunity glowingly described her project. At the Theosophical Convention of 1898 in Chicago she elaborated her scheme by submitting a new constitution which was dutifully adopted by the society in spite of the withdrawal of several dissenting groups. The society's name became "The Universal Brotherhood and Theosophical Society," and Mrs. Tingley assumed autocratic powers with the right to choose her own successor.

Before Katherine Tingley had time to build her international headquarters in California, the Spanish-American War broke out, and the philanthropist sensed immediate work to be done. Her first efforts aided wounded and diseased veterans stationed on Long Island. More significant, however, to the future settlement in California, she recruited a relief expedition to Cuba in February, 1899, after the end of hostilities. While on the island, she developed a special interest in Cuban children and later attracted seventy-five of them to Point Loma where they became an integral part of her school.

At the Convention of 1898, Katherine Tingley invited individual Theosophists to join her in building the community at Point Loma, a work seriously under way by 1900. For the next twenty-nine years until her death, she devoted the largest share of her energies to the development of the 330 acres. She ruled a domain which in its heyday, around 1907, included a population of five hundred, three large buildings—two surmounted by aquamarine and amethyst-glass domes which were illuminated at night—groups of smaller bungalows and tents used as dwellings, a Greek theater, forty-foot avenues winding through luxuriant gardens and orchards, and forests of eucalyptus planted on previously unwooded ground.

Point Loma presented as good an example of a religious utopia as can be found in California history, but Katherine Tingley did not conceive of it as such. She looked upon the Universal Brotherhood, not as a socialistic or utopian colony, but as the practical translation of the teachings of Theosophy into concrete form.[13] Other Theosophists, too, sought to correct any false ideas that might associate Point Loma with nineteenth-century utopianism:

> Of the many attempts to form settlements and colonies some were no doubt started on lines of unselfish endeavour, and as Katherine Tingley has said—if they had only had the basis of Theosophy they might have proved a success. But mere good intention and unselfish ideals are not enough, and it was the knowledge of life and human nature which alone Theosophy gives which was lacking.[14]

Theosophists objected to calling Point Loma utopian because they looked upon their experiment, unlike others, as the demonstration of a true formula. But few utopian colonies ever existed which did not claim this same qualification, and certainly every utopian colony, religious or secular, could have adopted the definition with which Katherine Tingley described Point Loma as "a practical illustration of the possibility of developing a higher type of humanity."[15]

[13]Tingley, *Life at Point Loma*, p. 6. The word "colony" is used in this chapter synonymously with "community." The latter term was preferred by the members at Point Loma, but it is hoped that the occasional use of the former here will give no offense.

[14]*International Theosophical Chronicle* (London and N.Y.), III (March, 1907), 75.

[15]*Life at Point Loma*, p. 17.

By 1903 the membership in the settlement had reached three hundred, nearly half of which were children in the schools. From that time the number grew more slowly till it reached about five hundred around 1910.[16] Most of the members represented middle-class or upper-middle-class backgrounds and were on the whole well-educated. The greatest number came from local Theosophical lodges throughout the United States and a sprinkling from European branches, especially England and Sweden. A few wealthy businessmen played an important role by managing the community's financial affairs. Two of the most prominent of these financiers were Albert G. Spalding, founder of the sporting goods firm of A. G. Spalding and Brothers, and William Chase Temple, Pittsburgh promoter and Florida fruitgrower. Others included Clark Thurston, former president of the American Screw Company, and W. Ross White, Georgia manufacturer.

Only a few years after the founding, Katherine Tingley tangled with the press. Harrison Gray Otis, editor of the Los Angeles *Times* and a man deeply concerned with California's reputation, heartily disapproved of fanatical cults, a category in which he placed the Theosophists at Point Loma. On October 28, 1901, he exultantly published in the *Times* an account by an "escaped" member of the colony and headlined the story, "Outrages at Point Loma . . . Startling Tales Told . . . Women and Children Starved." He labeled Point Loma "the spookery," a term he used consistently thereafter to designate the colony, and described it as a "place of horror" surrounded by armed men under the "strong hypnotic power" of Katherine Tingley. "The poor children are . . . continually on the verge of starvation. . . ." "Gross immoralities are practiced" as when "on certain occasions a mid-

---

[16]Most visitors agreed substantially on these estimates. See Charles F. Lummis, "In the Lion's Den," *Out West*, XVII (Dec., 1902), 738; Bertha D. Knobe, "The Point Loma Community," *Munsey's Magazine*, XXIX (June, 1903), 358; and Baker, "Extraordinary Experiment," *American*, LXIII (Jan., 1907), 230. See also William A. Hinds, *American Communities* (Chicago, 1908), p. 467. The Universal Brotherhood reported in U. S. Bureau of the Census, *Religious Bodies: 1926* (2 vols., Washington, D.C., 1930), I, 286-87, a total membership of 50,000, but this figure included unattached members throughout the world and no separate figures were given for Point Loma.

night pilgrimage is made by both men and women to a spot on the peninsula, which is termed sacred ground. They go in their night robes. . . ." Mrs. Tingley was understandably furious and immediately brought suit for libel. On January 12, 1903, a jury awarded her $7,500.[17]

In the midst of the libel case arrived more troublous news. Immigration officials had quarantined eleven Cuban children from five to ten years of age who, accompanied by Gertrude W. van Pelt, had been en route to Point Loma. The Society for the Prevention of Cruelty to Children had claimed that the Point Loma school was financially and morally incompetent to care for the children, who were therefore likely to become public charges. For five weeks the press capitalized on the sensational story.[18] After extensive inquiries and a personal investigation of Point Loma by Commissioner of Immigration Frank P. Sargent, the government dismissed the case and permitted the children to resume their journey.

The Cubans represented only one type of recruitment for Point Loma. They had been specifically chosen by Katherine Tingley's representatives to take part in the educational program. Any person, however, who endorsed Theosophy might be accepted into the colony on probation after he had signed an agreement to abide by the rules and had paid an admission fee of $500 for himself and his family. Actually the fee varied considerably; wealthy members gave much more, and poorer, less or nothing. The tuition in the school ranged from no fee to $2,000 annually.

Members received no wages for their labor. They worked at tasks assigned them by Mrs. Tingley through her General Manager. Jobs rotated and the tasks were varied as often as possible. Residents did not provide a sufficient labor supply for all needs, however, and certain tasks, like new construction, had to be

[17]Los Angeles *Times*, Jan. 13, 1903. Her victory did not go unobserved by other editors. When in 1917 the Oakland *Tribune* printed a story considered by Tingley to be libelous, the editor quickly admitted an injustice, paid Tingley $5,000, and published an apology. San Diego *Union*, June 26, 1917.

[18]San Francisco *Chronicle*, Nov. 1, 2, 3, 4, 13, 19, Dec. 7, 8, 15, 1902. Los Angeles *Times*, Nov. 13, 16, 22, 23, 1902.

hired out. The women of the community manufactured practically all of the clothing, a chore simplified by the fact that the men wore uniforms and the women dressed in simple, if not identical, garments.

Those engaged in the agricultural branch of the colony had reason to be proud of their efforts. Under the direction of Orange and Abbott Clark, its chief horticulturists, the community achieved remarkable records of fruit production and pioneered in experimentation with avocados and tropical fruits which contributed materially to the agricultural development of the state. By 1910 the members raised about one half of their food supply.[19]

The capitalist concept of private property remained undisturbed. Wealthy members were never forced to abandon worldly holdings. The lands and properties of the community were held in the name of various corporations, the control of which rested in each case with Katherine Tingley.[20] As with Thomas Lake Harris, Mrs. Tingley conceived of her holdings as a trust for the group as a whole. Resident members had little need for money. The community took care of most costs from doctor's to plumber's bills. For any unusual requirements, such as necessary trips, money could be requisitioned, but the practice was not widespread.

Members lived either in the large communal Homestead or in individual bungalows scattered over the grounds. Married couples, too, could choose between bungalow or Homestead. A rambling refectory served communal meals, with two dining

[19]California Avocado Assn. *Yearbook* (Los Angeles, 1928), p. 44, presented a detailed analysis of the 123,158 pounds of fruit (including over 43,000 pounds of oranges and 20,000 pounds of avocados), and 2,552 pounds of honey produced at Point Loma each year. Ernest Braunton, as associate editor of the *California Cultivator*, LXXIII (Oct. 5, 1929), 332, praised the Point Loma horticulturists for their scientific care and experimentation. For food supply figures see *Raja Yoga Messenger*, VI (Sept. 25, 1910), 12-13.

[20]Lomaland Properties, the most important of these corporations, held most of the land and assets other than the school. See the circular for its bond issue of 1927, Archives of the Theosophical Society, Pasadena. The school, as a non-profit, educational institution, was incorporated separately in order to avoid taxation of its land and buildings.

rooms for the adults and a separate room for the children. The relative numbers of married and unmarried people in the community apparently differed little from external society. Marriage, at any rate, was a common and frequent event, although no particular Theosophical ceremony was prescribed. Just as Theosophists could belong to any traditional church, so they could be married with any preferred church ritual or simply by the justice of the peace in San Diego. Sometimes the Rev. S. J. Niell, a resident of the colony, conducted rites in the glass-domed Temple. On one occasion he married six couples in a single ceremony.

Visitors reported the general tone of the community as military with strict order, discipline, and saluting. Photographs of members surf-bathing and golfing seem to belie a rigorous routine, but the boys drilled each morning, occasionally engaged in martial maneuvers, and wore, along with the men, decidedly military uniforms.[21]

The family units did not include children. Parents deposited their offspring a few months after birth in a communal nursery, seeing them regularly thereafter only on Sundays. Between the age of three and four the child moved from the nursery into a dormitory. Here he learned to make his own bed, to dress himself, and in general to accept communal responsibility. Furthermore, at this early age he embarked on musical training and visited for short periods the classrooms of the older children. After reaching school age, he joined the older boys or girls living in groups of ten in separate circular-shaped bungalows. A teacher resided with each group day and night, and the ten or twelve rooms in these dormitories radiated like spokes from a central sitting room so that the master might have constant surveillance over each of his charges. After 1904 the girls moved into the Homestead while the boys remained in the group houses.

[21]E. H. von Wiegand, "Mystics, Babies, and Bloom," *Sunset*, XXIII (Aug., 1909), 118. B. D. Knobe, "Point Loma Community," *Munsey's Magazine*, XXIX (June, 1903), 362. In addition to the countless pictures of the school in the early issues of the *Theosophical Path*, a good set of photographs taken by an outsider and non-Theosophist, Charles F. Lummis, is in *Out West*, XVIII (Jan., 1903), 35-48.

The students spent only two and a half hours a day in actual class work. English and foreign languages, arithmetic, history—all were taught, and in spite of the short hours a surprising degree of proficiency resulted. Public demonstrations of the achievements of the pupils impressed audiences in San Diego.[22] Sometimes outside visitors were permitted to question the children freely. Ray Stannard Baker, an editor of the *American Magazine* and later biographer of Woodrow Wilson, when given such an opportunity wished to test the colony's intellectual isolation and therefore asked a boy of fourteen to discuss governmental railroad regulation in the United States. The lad presented a summary of the problem and concluded that the fundamental difficulty lay in the selfishness of men; the only solution, in the application of brotherhood. The antidote, although undeniably applicable to any social problem, indicates clearly the tenor of the boy's schooling.[23]

Only a small percentage of the pupils were children of colony residents. The largest number of paying students were sent by Theosophists all over the United States who wished their progeny to be trained in the doctrines. Among the non-paying students were a large number brought by Katherine Tingley in 1901 from an orphan and settlement house in Buffalo. In the same year she sent three representatives to Cuba to gather thirty-five children from six to fourteen years of age, a minority of whom paid tuition at Point Loma. These Cuban children were already at the Point when their eleven compatriots, as we have seen, were detained in New York in 1902. The next largest foreign group came from Sweden where Katherine Tingley on her World Crusade had established strong local units. All told, the school at Point Loma averaged three hundred children with sixty-five instructors. Most of the younger teachers were trained at Point

[22]See San Diego *Union*, Aug. 16, 23, Sept. 6, 13, 16, 20, and 23, 1915, for one such series.

[23]Baker, "Extraordinary Experiment," *American Magazine*, LXIII (Jan., 1907), 229. For another visitor's favorable comments on the school, see Charles F. Lummis, "In the Lion's Den," *Out West*, XVII (Dec., 1902), 737.

Loma, but a sizable proportion, especially of those teaching on the higher grade-levels, were specially recruited, like Professor Frederick Dick, from among educated Theosophists wherever Katherine Tingley met them.

Mrs. Tingley called her school the Raja Yoga, a term which she had read in Sanskrit literature, meaning "kingly union," the perfect balance of all the faculties, physical, mental, and spiritual. She assumed the essential divinity of the child yet cautioned against the emergence of his brutish nature.[24] Thus the child underwent constant supervision, day and night, to guard against the outcroppings of evil. Stemming from the Theosophic doctrines of Karma and Reincarnation, this careful surveillance paved the way for the upward progress of the soul. Brotherhood and co-operation were vital in achieving a higher level of incarnation; therefore, the child learned that gossip was moral murder and the good of the whole community must transcend his own personal desires.

The children at Point Loma enjoyed unusual opportunities in the fine arts. At an early age they began training in voice and piano, learning theory on false, wooden keyboards. Orchestras flourished. The beginner entered the preparatory orchestra, which labored with four sections of violins. The school orchestra absorbed the better students and often performed on public occasions. Still more advanced, the Raja Yoga International Orchestra admitted only the most trained or talented musicians. In 1916, after guest-conducting the latter group in a work of Sibelius, Walter Damrosch, director of the New York Symphony Orchestra, highly praised the organization and concluded "that music is a part of your daily lives."[25]

The Theosophists at Point Loma stamped a deep cultural im-

[24]Tingley, *Voice of the Soul*, p. 81, and *Life at Point Loma*, p. 8.

[25]*Theosophical Path*, X (June, 1916), 618. For the visit and comments of Madame Melba see *ibid.*, XII (April, 1917), 429. For glowing praise from Alfred Hertz, Wagnerian conductor of the Metropolitan Opera House, see *ibid.*, XI (July, 1916), 102. Grace F. Knoche, born and raised at Point Loma, considers the music and the drama the most wonderful influences of her childhood; interview with the author, Feb. 27, 1952.

pression on San Diego dramatically as well as musically. The amphitheater, one of the earliest structures ordered by Katherine Tingley, was the first Greek theater in California.[26] With eleven semi-circular tiers of seats, it accommodated twenty-five hundred people who looked across a mosaic pavement, through "a chaste little temple in pure Greek architecture," to the open sea. In 1901, Mrs. Tingley purchased the Fisher Opera House in San Diego, which she renamed the Isis Theater. Here she presented devotional programs on Sunday evenings as well as restagings for the general public of dramatic spectacles from the Greek Theater.

She chose for the first epic the *Eumenides* of Aeschylus, finding in the inexorable pursuit of Orestes by the Furies clear reflections of the law of Karma. Though the repertory expanded, *Eumenides* retained its fascination in revival after revival. Shakespeare also provided a favorite vehicle; in the quarter of a century of Katherine Tingley's leadership, lavish productions of *Midsummer Night's Dream, As You Like It, Merry Wives of Windsor, The Tempest*, and *Twelfth Night* echoed within the Greek Theater or livened the stage of the Isis.[27] Sheldon Cheney, founder and editor of *Theater Arts Magazine*, referred to the Point Loma productions as "a new art form, a sort of decorative drama that is more dependent upon the visual beauty of costumes, natural setting, grouping and dancing, and upon incidental poetry, than upon sustained emotional appeal."[28]

From the standpoint of community life, the performances were gigantic co-operative efforts. The entire population took part from Madame Tingley herself who directed to the nursery child who pasted paper flowers on a garland. Miss Grace Knoche remembers to this day her excitement as a child at being chosen to portray Mustardseed in *Midsummer Night's Dream*. The programs carried no actors' names; all work was anonymous.

[26]Sheldon Cheney, *The Open-Air Theater* (N.Y., 1918), p. 36.

[27]For a sampling of reviews of these plays see San Diego *Union*, April 18, 1899, March 24, 1907, July 20, 1915, Feb. 8, 1916, and June 22, 1917.

[28]*Open-Air Theater*, p. 37.

But the contagious enthusiasm spread far beyond the footlights, as the newspaper reviews so clearly indicate.

Sympathetic coverage on the part of the San Diego *Union*, a paper which seemed genuinely impressed with the whole program at Point Loma, contrasted vividly with the deep hostility issuing from other powerful outsiders. The extent to which Otis and the Los Angeles *Times* sought to besmirch the name of the colony has already been noted. The Los Angeles *Herald* usually upheld the Tingley experiment, mostly to spite its mortal rival, the *Times*.[29] Enough of the people of San Diego were sufficiently sympathetic with the Theosophists to fill the Isis Theater Sunday night after Sunday night and to consistently patronize the musical and theatrical events on the Point. Tourists and visitors became so bothersome at the community that an admission fee of ten cents was charged partly to discourage their numbers. A Theosophical Information Bureau in the U. S. Grant Hotel, San Diego's largest, kept some of the idly curious away by answering questions, as well as dispensing tickets for the productions. One powerful element of antagonism, however, arose from the clergy of San Diego. On August 21, 1901, twenty clergymen, representing both Catholic and Protestant denominations, published a denunciation of Theosophy, calling it "destructive alike of aspiration and hope" and "diametrically opposed to the Gospel of Christ."[30] The remainder of the month was consumed with challenges and debates and countercharges between the members at Point Loma and the clergy of San Diego, with no results more edifying than a lingering suspicion on both sides.

Whether it was directing the *Eumenides* or planning a dormitory, the real administration and government of Point Loma stemmed from Katherine Tingley. She openly affirmed: "The government of the Universal Brotherhood and Theosophical Society is autocratic and rests entirely in the hands of the Leader

[29]See, for example, Los Angeles *Herald*, Dec. 8, 13, 1901, and Nov. 16, Dec. 21, 1902.

[30]San Diego *Union*, Aug. 21, 1901.

and Official Head."[31] The constitution named Katherine A. Tingley as the Leader for life and granted her the power to choose her successor, to appoint and remove all lesser officers, to declare policy, and to direct all affairs. Madame Tingley was no democrat. "There is a top rung to every ladder," she wrote, and she frankly assigned herself that position in the Theosophical hierarchy.[32]

She appointed a cabinet of thirteen men, who were enjoined by the constitution to promulgate the measures of the Leader. These men directed financial affairs, a task which Mrs. Tingley carefully avoided in order to deflect any possible charges of corruption on her part.

She was wise to be careful, for the finances of the community were open to question. Any outsider could sense lavish expenditures after a brief look at the elaborate buildings or the frequent theatrical and musical extravaganzas. Businessmen evaluated the building improvements alone at over $300,000.[33]

The theatrical performances brought some return, however, although undoubtedly not a profit. Admission for the general public started at seventy-five cents and ran up to two dollars with boxes at ten dollars. Audiences often averaged over a thousand, hence the productions were probably no great financial drain, if a drain at all. Tuition from the school provided some revenue in spite of the number of children who were supported free.[34]

[31]*Life at Point Loma*, p. 4.

[32]"Constitution of the Universal Brotherhood," Archives of Theosophical Society, Pasadena. The quotation is from *Life at Point Loma*, p. 7.

[33]Circular advertising bond issue of 1927, Los Angeles, in Archives of Theosophical Society, Pasadena. This circular was prepared by Bayly Bros., an investment underwriting firm of Los Angeles. Estimates in the circular were made by Mr. John C. Cain, appraiser for the Merchants National Trust and Savings Bank of Los Angeles.

[34]*Theosophical Forum*, VIII (June, 1936), 474. It should be remembered that the teachers served without pay. Tingley estimated in 1924 that from the beginning the school had completely educated and cared for 37% of the children; partially another 37%; and at full tuition, only 26%. *Theosophical Path*, XXVII (Sept., 1924), 291. Gertrude W. van Pelt stated that from its opening to 1913 the school had entirely supported 152 children for periods from one to fifteen years and had partly supported 72 others. *Ibid.*, V (July, 1913), 50.

The substantial income at Point Loma, however, flowed from contributions. Much of this came in the form of direct gift. In 1929 Katherine Tingley's successor publicly announced receipt of $100,000 in gifts since her death.[35] On other occasions wealthy members lent the community large sums with promissory notes for collateral. In 1927, $239,000 was outstanding in this form.[36] Legacies from deceased members provided further income. The community received $140,000 from the estate of Harriet Patterson Thurston alone.[37] In addition to donations, the colony profited from an increase in land values. By 1927 the 330 acres were evaluated at $1,320,000.[38] Beginning around 1926 Katherine Tingley sold blocks of land, sometimes for as high as $5,000 an acre.[39]

Nevertheless, the excess of outlay over income continued. The Mohn Case, in which Mrs. Irene Mohn charged Mrs. Tingley with alienation of the affections of her husband, George Mohn, cost Mrs. Tingley $100,000 and lowered the prestige of the community incalculably.[40] Under Mrs. Tingley's autocratic regime unnecessary expenditures, such as underground electrical wiring, persisted. In 1927 indebtedness required the floating of a $400,000 bond issue.

Thus the financial situation looked menacing when on July 11, 1929, the community sorrowfully announced to the world the accidental death of its leader. At seventy-nine years of age, she had died in Europe where she had been inspecting the work of the local lodges inaugurated on the World Crusade of 1896-97. Within a few weeks the society announced her chosen successor as Gottfried de Purucker, whom she had first met on the World Crusade, who had lived at Point Loma from the beginning, and

[35]San Diego *Union*, Aug. 3, 1929.

[36]Circular for bond issue of 1927.

[37]Orange *News* (Orange, Calif.), Jan. 5, 1915.

[38]Circular for bond issue of 1927.

[39]San Diego *Union*, Dec. 19, 1926.

[40]San Diego *Union*, July 10, 1923.

who had achieved wide recognition in the interpretation and publication of Sanskrit literature.

The new leader embarked on an ambitious program, but the onset of the depression paralyzed its fulfillment. The financial situation, already critical before 1929, steadily worsened. Drastic retrenchments cut costs to a bare minimum, making survival possible for twelve years after Katherine Tingley's death. But the glory of the community had faded.

By 1940 the creditors had been satisfied through the sale of all land except the acres immediately surrounding the central buildings. With the advent of World War II, the movement of greater military installations into the area, and the consequent demand for wartime housing, the community liquidated its remaining holdings and moved debt-free to a secluded spot amid the orange groves of Covina. Theosophical leaders no longer conceived of their task as the practical demonstration of Theosophy in community form; their efforts were now directed toward expansion of the local lodges and an increased emphasis on publication. But the glass domes of the Homestead and Temple gleaming until recently on the Point Loma headlands could remind San Diegans of days when Katherine Tingley ruled a fabulous realm of cultured co-operation, an economic socialism in only a few aspects, but a co-operative utopia in many.

In 1898 as the Theosophical Society in America splintered under the impact of Katherine Tingley's accession, the leaders of the Theosophical lodge in Syracuse, New York, received mystical instructions from the Great White Brotherhood to secede from the Tingley-tainted society. The true Theosophical order, the revelations said, must be carried on in a direct line from the founding work of Helena Blavatsky. William H. Dower, a medical doctor, and Mrs. Francia A. LaDue, co-receptors of the message, consequently instituted the Temple of the People. The two founders led their group westward in 1903, settled in a fertile coastal valley near Pismo Beach, and appropriately named their new headquarters Halcyon.

As Madame Tingley concentrated on a school, William Dower, understandably as a doctor, looked to the building of a sanatorium. On May 25, 1904, a three-story frame building with gables, bays, parapets, and copious Victorian gingerbread was formally opened. Dr. Dower welcomed a gathering for the ceremonies, described the projected work as an attempt to inculcate love and harmony in order to conquer all abnormality and disease, and impressed the assembly with a demonstration of the sanatorium's new and miraculous X-ray machine.

The sanatorium, however, represented only the physical road to the regeneration of mankind; political, economic, and social paths were not ignored. A portion of the Temple organized into a co-operative colony and incorporated this separate venture in 1905 as the Temple Home Association. A membership fee of $100 entitled the individual to one vote. He might make an additional investment, which would yield him larger dividends when the profits warranted, but in no case could he buy more than a single vote. The aim of the association was to create a community "wherein all the land will be owned all of the time by all of the people; where all the means of production and distribution, tools, machinery, and natural resources, will be owned by the people—the community—and where Capital and Labor may meet on equal terms with no special privileges to either."[41] As Theosophists of an earlier generation had embraced Nationalism, so many members at Temple Home looked favorably on the cause of socialism, finding Eugene Debs and Upton Sinclair moving in the same direction as Theosophy. One member wrote, "While [all] Socialists are not Theosophists, I have a feeling that all Theosophists should be Socialists."[42]

The government of Temple Home was not, however, as democratic as in most strictly socialist colonies. A board of three directors was elected by the voting members of the association, Dr. Dower and Mrs. LaDue being unanimously chosen year after

[41] *Temple Artisan*, VIII (July, 1907), 36.

[42] R. W. Northey, in *ibid.*, VII (Jan., 1907), 158. See also a letter on socialism from J. Varian, *ibid.*, IX (Aug., 1908), 48-50.

year to fill two of the places. The membership met on the first Monday evening of each month, but the recommendations of this meeting had no binding power on the Board of Directors.

Workers in the colony received their living expenses plus ten dollars a month. Each member acquired one half of an acre to work on his own account. The colony grew vegetables and grains, such as oats and barley, and early developed profitable crops of sugar beets and flower seeds. In periods of cultivation and harvest the hiring of local Japanese supplemented the labor of members.

Within a few years the colony numbered fifty people.[43] Family units were undisturbed and the children tramped each day to the public schools in the town of Arroyo Grande. At least once in each month the entire colony planned an outing, swimming in the surf or picnicking or digging for Pismo clams.

By 1908 the *Temple Artisan*, a monthly magazine of the Temple of the People which also included news of the Temple Home Association, gave evidence, if sometimes veiled, of internal conflict. "We would not be on a human basis if there were not a splash of friction occasionally here and there between workers—but this is soon adjusted by the inflow of Lodge light and force ever welling from the real Temple Heart."[44] The same issue and that of the following May printed open letters imploring members not to heed the current rumors and criticism. Confronted with such troubles and a financial stringency, which had slowly intensified through the years, in 1912 the Board of Directors recommended a revision of the Temple Home Association. All mortgages would be retired by the sale of available property; the actively co-operative work of the colony would cease; and the Temple Home Association would become no more than a land-holding adjunct to the Temple of the People. By 1913 all

[43]This figure comes from the *Temple Artisan*, IX (Dec., 1908), 134. William A. Hinds in his *American Communities* (2nd revision, Chicago, 1908), p. 577, a work of which Temple Home thought highly and distributed through its book concern, listed the membership in 1906 at 140. This number probably represented the inclusive congregation of the Temple of the People rather than the smaller co-operative experiment of Temple Home.

[44]*Temple Artisan*, VIII (Jan., 1908), 155.

of the recommendations had gone into effect, and the economic aspects of the venture in utopia had ended. Technically the Temple Home still operates, selling memberships for $100 which entitle the member to perpetual use of one-half acre of land. The parent religious body in 1952 owned about 100 acres on which lived approximately seventy-five resident members. Cottages still encircle the six or seven central community buildings, while the old sanitorium stands a short distance away, deteriorating into a forbidding Victorian skeleton.[45]

[45]Another Theosophical colony, which had, however, few utopian or communitarian overtones beyond those of a group with a common philosophy, was Krotona, established by Albert P. Warrington on fifteen acres of the Hollywood hills in 1911. Faced with the increase of population in and around Hollywood, he moved the colony in 1924 to Ojai, where its members still live atop Krotona Hill to the south of town. Warrington owed allegiance to the Adyar branch of Theosophy, hence he sympathized and communicated little with either Point Loma or Temple Home.

CHAPTER 4

The Icaria Speranza
Commune

E ARLY in 1881 the heads of two French families, Armand Dehay and Jules Leroux, reconnoitered the Napa and Sonoma Valleys in search of the proper location for a utopian experiment. In September the men purchased a fertile tract three miles south of Cloverdale on the banks of the Russian River, some fifty miles north of San Francisco Bay. The Cloverdale *Reveille* on September 24, 1881, reported the sale as "885 acres of the best kind of land for vineyard and orchard." The country was hilly with gentle slopes breaking into the higher ridges of the Coast Range to the east. The Bank of California sold the property for $15,000.[1] The Dehay and Leroux families moved over the forty miles from St. Helena; several French families, including the Bées and the Provosts, gathered from San Francisco; and the community was ready to embark upon its corporate existence.

Local newspapers referred to the new settlement as the French Colony, but few understood the long, tragic background and the complicated set of principles which had brought these families to the Sonoma foothills. Two types of French utopianism lay at the roots of the colony. Armand Dehay, among others, represented a persistent series of attempts to embody on earth the

---

[1] The land was that part of the Rancho Rincon de Musalacon owned by the Bluxome family. It actually consisted of 885½ acres. Deed in Recorder's Office, Sonoma County Courthouse, Santa Rosa, Calif. Five years earlier, the families could have bought a portion of the land at tax sale for $47.75; *Sonoma Democrat* (Santa Rosa), Supplement, Feb. 5, 1876.

ideals of the French utopia, Icaria; Jules Leroux and his sons brought to California, in addition to Icarian principles, the tenets of Henri Saint-Simon. Saint-Simonianism accounted for few colony experiments, but it called for economic planning by scientists or technicians. Icaria, a controlled economy, nevertheless was based on democratic decision rather than the dictatorship of Saint-Simon's scientific planners.

Icarianism, the more dominant background in the new community, had sprung originally from the mind of Etienne Cabet, whose novel, *Voyage en Icarie*, had captured the imagination of mid-nineteenth-century revolutionary France.[2] Cabet, an environmentalist like most utopian socialists, held that men suffered vice and misfortune only because society was poorly organized. Inequality, the basic social evil, could be abolished only through a system of communism, a community of goods, which Cabet saw feasible for the first time in history as a result of modern production and industrial development. These ideas were hardly original, but Cabet's picturization of them in Icaria and his dramatic call for the immediate realization of that picture produced for him a solid and sizable following.

Sixty-nine Frenchmen became sufficiently enthusiastic to join

[2]Etienne Cabet, *Voyage en Icarie* (2 vols., Paris, 1840; 3rd ed., 1848). Etienne Cabet, born at Dijon, France, 1788, studied medicine before he turned to law. In Paris during the Restoration he was a member of the revolutionary Charbonnière. His appointment as Procurer-General of Corsica was revoked because of his writings against the French Charter. During the same year he was elected deputy from Dijon, having been openly supported by the radical *Aide-toi* society. In this period he wrote his history of the Revolution of 1830 and founded a radical paper, *Populaire*. In 1834 he was condemned to two years in jail for an article on Poland, but he escaped to England where he continued his pamphlet warfare against the government of Louis Philippe. Following his return to France under the Amnesty of 1839, his communist ideas began to manifest themselves beginning with his *Histoire de la Révolution de 1789 à 1830*. *Voyage en Icarie* appeared in 1840; admittedly it proceeded from ideas of Saint-Simon, Fourier, Owen, and Babeuf. *Populaire* was revived as an Icarian journal, Icarian courses were organized, and an *Almanach Icarien* was published frequently to spread the new brand of communism. Following 1847, all of Cabet's ideas converged in the project for Icarian colonization in America. Adolphe Robert and E. B. Cougny, *Dictionnaire des Parlementaires Français* (5 vols., Paris, 1891); Jules Prudhommeaux, *Icarie et son Fondateur Etienne Cabet* (Paris, 1907), hereafter cited as Prudhommeaux, *Icarie*.

Cabet as the *avant-garde* of the movement to plant in 1848 a new utopia on the banks of the Red River in Texas. Literally thousands of Frenchmen planned to follow the initial move, but before they had come, sickness, a nefarious land company, and inadequate preparation combined to reduce the glorious *garde* to a thin trickle of disappointed men and women staggering back to New Orleans to meet their newly arrived chief. Cabet, inspiring new resolution, led the group up the Mississippi to Nauvoo, Illinois. Here in the abandoned Mormon village stood a community ready-made: farms and dwellings and communal buildings. Even after losing twenty of their number to cholera on the river-journey, 260 Icarians arrived at Nauvoo in March, 1849. They rented 450 acres of land, later bought much of it, and by the end of 1850 they owned a steam mill, distillery, malt house, farm appurtenances, and they had opened stores in St. Louis to sell the surplus product of shoemaker and tailor.

During the first half of the decade beginning in 1850 Icaria came closest to its dream of material and spiritual success. Nearly five hundred members took part in a community life which included an orchestra, a theatrical group enacting scenes from *Andromaque* and *Le Cid*, and a library of some six thousand volumes.

Yet all was not well in utopia. In the early 1850's political and financial conditions deteriorated. Before this time in the flush of enthusiasm, Cabet had conveyed his temporary dictatorial powers back to the community. As the financial situation became progressively more serious toward the end of 1855, he sought to regain some of these powers through a four-year presidential term. The Icarian constitution had expressly forbidden constitutional revision except at two-year intervals falling in the month of March.[3] Cabet's proposed revision crystallized the latent hostilities of six years of communal living and divided the community clearly into hostile camps. As the months went by, "Cabetistes" refused to eat at the table with "dissidents," the pro-Cabet minority

[3]"Constitution de la Communauté Icarienne," in Prudhommeaux, *Icarie*, p. 631.

struck and rioted, the anti-Cabet majority in turn burned Cabet's books in protest and eventually expelled the founder. His loyal followers moved with him into exile and together established a new community, Cheltenham, near St. Louis. But Cabet did not long survive the expulsion; he died on November 8, 1856, and was buried in St. Louis. The Cheltenham group slowly dissolved, many of its members returning to the central fold at Nauvoo.

The next Icarian utopia evolved not far away—in Iowa. Cabet himself early foresaw the advantages of a more isolated position; perhaps he even took a cue from the bitter experiences of his Mormon predecessors in Nauvoo. At any rate as early as 1852, the Icarians bought government land in southwestern Iowa. In 1857 eighteen men were already improving the 3,115 Iowa acres, cultivating 273 of them.[4] The community schism and the national depression of 1857 left the Nauvoo group weak and tottering. The land along the Mississippi was sold for debt and a fresh start projected as the Icarians moved to the Iowa frontier. Hardships multiplied; the debt seemed insurmountable because of depression prices and difficulties with transportation and marketing. With the Civil War, however, came relief; crop prices boomed; and by 1868 Icaria was solvent and numbered sixty members. Ten years later the population had expanded to eighty-three with fifty applications for membership on hand.[5] Life was even gay: sleigh rides, skating parties and dances, swimming and fishing parties in summer, and always the grand fête ball of February 3 to commemorate the sailing of the *avant-garde* from Le Havre.

Again, however, storms brewed for the band of idealists. Newly admitted members had stood at the barricades during the Paris Commune, and they injected far more radical ideas than some of the older Icarians could accept. Increased dissidence arose over such insignificant details as individual *petits jardins*, denounced by the younger radicals as entering wedges of private

[4]Albert Shaw, *Icaria: A Chapter in the History of Communism* (N.Y., 1884), p. 76. Hereafter cited as Shaw, *Icaria*.

[5]President Sauva's statement of 1877, Hinds, *American Communities* (2nd ed., Chicago, 1902), p. 342.

ownership. These superficial quarrels concealed a more basic cleavage, however, and in 1878 the factions decided to separate. The more conservative party moved a few miles south, dragging its houses on runners behind oxen over wintry soil, and left the more radical group, which now named itself "Jeune Icarie," to pursue its new ideas alone. The conservatives set up a "New Icaria" and remained in a weakened state of existence till 1898, long after the Jeune Icarie and California colonies had succumbed. In this sense the New Icarians can be called the last of the Icarians. Their bitterness over the split of 1878 did not subside and they had little to do with their former associates whether in Iowa or California.

CHART OF ICARIAN COMMUNITIES

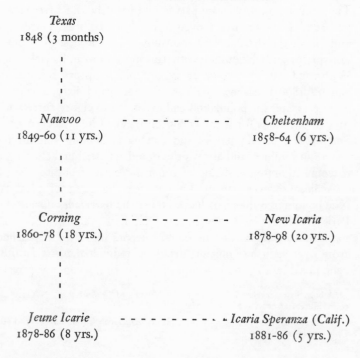

Texas
1848 (3 months)

Nauvoo   - - - - - - - - - -   *Cheltenham*
1849-60 (11 yrs.)   1858-64 (6 yrs.)

Corning   - - - - - - - - - -   *New Icaria*
1860-78 (18 yrs.)   1878-98 (20 yrs.)

Jeune Icarie   - - - - - - - - - - ⤵ *Icaria Speranza* (Calif.)
1878-86 (8 yrs.)   1881-86 (5 yrs.)

Meanwhile Jeune Icarie, like all Icarias, remained a purely French settlement, with native tongue maintained in all journals and records, education, and social intercourse. A system of communal property prevailed. New members underwent a six-months' trial novitiate, definitive membership being granted at the end of that time by vote of the General Assembly. This democratic body, composed of all members, held supreme power, more power, indeed, than similar assemblies in previous Icarias; for Jeune Icarie had abolished the office of president, and the executive function was handled by a board of four trustees elected annually by the assembly.

During its first year the outlook for Jeune Icarie seemed bright. From thirty-five at the time of the split, the membership rose to seventy-five by the fall of 1880. The debt in October, 1879, decreased to $4,000. An Icarian forge and shoe-shop opened in Corning. The fêtes were gay; the community theater was reorganized; and the orchestra was sufficiently proficient and popular to be hired by neighboring villages.

Among the new applicants for membership in this period of prosperity were Armand Dehay and his family. Dehay had a purpose in mind when he petitioned for admission in May, 1879. He wanted to test himself and his family in the theory and practices of communal living. At this time he was thirty-seven years old, married, with four of his eventual nine children. The move from Corning where Armand had pursued his trade of barbering, out three miles into the agricultural setting of Icaria was not actually consummated until November. But during this half-year the community had anxiously awaited his coming, preparing to receive the family as early as June. The Dehays were known and loved in Icaria; Madame Dehay's father, Jules Leroux, venerated French communist exile, and the family of her elder brother, Paul, all lived in the community. The Dehays usually visited the utopian settlement on Sundays and on the Icarian festival days.

Armand Dehay had emigrated from France in the early 1870's and as a barber had worked in various eastern cities before moving westward to Kansas. Farming on the homestead of his friend and countryman, Jules Leroux, he married Jules's youngest daughter and followed the Leroux family to Iowa. He barbered the citizens of Corning for some years before joining forces with Icaria.

The optimistic air which Jeune Icarie breathed at the time Dehay sought admission vanished with the decade of the seventies. By the end of 1880 the debt had reached $7,000; the shops in Corning were closed, ostensibly because of need for farm hands and because it had been found "unwise for some members to be individualistically detached from the great family."[6] Forty acres of land were sold. Membership began to decline through frequent withdrawals until the community paper admitted, "Diminution of our numbers results in lodgings and work available for prospective members."[7] During 1881 the membership sank to thirty.

Under these conditions Armand Dehay and his family lived little more than six months in the community. He fulfilled his period of novitiate but did not apply for definitive membership, his reasons for not doing so being broadly theoretical as well as personal.

... Seeing that we cannot realize a beautiful and great community in Iowa because of the climate and the topographic situation of Icaria, and having passed from theory to practice, I am now more sure that I wish to help in the foundation of a communist colony in California or Texas where we can develop industry and export our products easily; and in my position as one who was formerly a tramp I propose to choose this happy country.

Another reason—and not the least—which determines me to leave you, is my wife's poor state of health. I think that in staying here she will fall further and further sick. It would be better to live in a more temperate country....[8]

Whether Dehay tramped to Texas in his search for a new locale is not known. He was, however, not the only member of Jeune Icarie to sense the advantages to utopia of a temperate climate. Several months after his departure, the colony dispatched a com-

[6]*La Jeune Icarie*, Dec. 31, 1880. [7]*Ibid.*, Aug.-Sept., 1880.
[8]*La Jeune Icarie*, June 15, 1880.

mittee to investigate localities in Florida.[9] Dehay meanwhile reached California and, writing of its attractions to his former comrades, he began to play on existing discontent within the shrinking Jeune Icarie to entice its remaining members to a California Icaria.

During 1881 Dehay was writing from St. Helena, Napa County, where he and his family probably stayed with his brother, Theodore. St. Helena was not far from San Francisco, and Armand may have been attracted to the Bay region by his friendship with men like Emile Bée, one of the leaders of the Socialist Labor Party in San Francisco. The affairs of the social radicals of this area had often been discussed in the pages of the community newspaper at Jeune Icarie. A former secretary of the Socialist Party in San Francisco had even sought membership in the Iowa community. Dehay thus was aware that the San Francisco population included friends congenial to his communal ideas.[10]

Socialist and labor groups in San Francisco were experiencing a flush of organizational awakening. Men like Dennis Kearney, leading vehement sand-lot agitation against capital and monopoly, were being replaced by organizers like Frank Roney, an avowed socialist who formed the Seamen's Protective Union in 1880. The Knights of Labor had nearly five thousand members in San Francisco around 1882. Labor had begun to send representatives to other national organizations, such as the Federation of Organized Trades and Labor-Unions, the incipient American Federation of Labor. Socialists were active in their own International Working-

---

[9] *L'Etoile des Pauvres*, Aug., 1881.

[10] See, for example, *La Jeune Icarie*, June 26 and Aug. 15, 1879, and Dec. 31, 1880. There seems to have existed an inexplicable rapport between southwestern Iowa and the Sonoma County area of California. At least the newspapers of the two areas seem to reflect such a relationship. In addition to the articles in *La Jeune Icarie* mentioned above, the *Sonoma Democrat* (Santa Rosa), July 3, 1875, carried the second letter of an exchange between a southwestern Iowa newspaper and the *Democrat*. The Adams County *Free Press* (Corning, Iowa) also carried a series of articles based on letters from the Sonoma County area: Nov. 23, 30, Dec. 7, 21, 1883.

men's Association, a provincial secret band, and in local units of the national Socialist Labor Party.

Emile Bée, friend of Armand Dehay, led one of the latter socialist locals. Bée was a French exile who had embraced revolutionary socialism as a tailor in Paris at the age of sixteen. He subscribed to the Icarian colonization funds of 1848, but during his first exile in 1851, instead of joining Icaria, he trekked to California to dig for gold. In 1871, after activity in the Paris Commune, he returned to San Francisco, and by 1881 he was leading an active section of the Socialist Labor Party.[11] When his friends Leroux and Dehay asked him to join them in setting up a co-operative colony, he undoubtedly received the suggestion as a real opportunity to practice his long-standing socialist theories.

Meanwhile the Dehays, examining California land, continued to write letters to Iowa which attracted Jules Leroux and his sons at Jeune Icarie to join them in St. Helena. Jules and his brother Pierre Leroux, as younger men in France, had both enthusiastically followed the social thinker Saint-Simon. Pierre had remained in France, a mystical, socialist philosopher, while Jules had emigrated to Kansas and homesteaded in 1867. It was on this homestead that Armand Dehay worked for Leroux and afterward married his youngest daughter. In 1877 Leroux's son, Paul, joined the Icarian community in Corning, Iowa, and shortly thereafter drew with him across the Kansas-Iowa border his father and mother, his brothers and sister, and Armand Dehay, his brother-in-law. Jules, the father, never became a member of the community but he lived among Icarians the rest of his life.

While Jules Leroux was still farming in Kansas, he had sold a part of his land and bought a hand printing press. His revolutionary ardor far from dead, he began the publication of a small, four-page monthly which he called, first, *L'Etoile du Kansas* and, after his move, *L'Etoile du Kansas et de l'Iowa*. He published the paper intermittently for the rest of his life, changing the name once more in California to *L'Etoile des Pauvres et des Souffrants*.

11Prudhommeaux, *Icarie*, p. 575.

Devoting his space largely to an exposition of his own ideas, he also printed correspondence from French and American socialists. He believed that Icarian socialism held no promise for mankind, and he virulently denounced Icarian withdrawal from the more active urban socialist world. But he enjoyed the Icarian hospitality, the Icarians revered him as a man of '48, and he later reciprocated by printing *La Jeune Icarie* for many years on his own press. On the last day of 1880 the paper sadly announced that Jules Leroux and his wife and their son, Paul, and his family were all leaving to join their relatives and friends in California and were taking the printing press with them. That was the last issue of *La Jeune Icarie.*

Early in 1881 the Leroux and Dehay families thus united in St. Helena and later in the same year organized their utopia near the village of Cloverdale. The initial group consisted of the families of Dehay, Leroux, Bée, and Gustave Provost, who had acted as representative in San Francisco for Jules Leroux's *L'Etoile* as early as 1879. At first they called their colony Speranza from the review *L'Esperance,* which Pierre Leroux had edited while in exile on the Island of Jersey during 1858-59. By the end of October these new owners of the Bluxome Ranch began construction of a sawmill to help clear the trees and prepare for the planting of vines.[12] The colony practiced communal living from the start but did not sign actual articles of agreement until several years later. Meanwhile they worked on plans for a merger with Jeune Icarie. Life in Speranza from 1881 to 1883 was a dressing of the ground for the real utopian experiment to come.

In the winter of 1883-84 the remaining Iowans at Jeune Icarie, in the face of their own rapidly diminishing membership and the persistently glowing letters from California, voted to pool resources and throw in their lot with the western Speranza. They elected Emile Peron and Emile Fugier as trustees for the liquidation, and thereupon most of the Iowa group, including Eugene Mourot and his family, the widow James, and young Alexis

[12]Cloverdale *Reveille,* Oct. 29, 1881.

Marchand, left for California. Late in 1883 the combined membership, those still in Iowa and those already in California, signed a Contract and Articles of Agreement. The following year they filed a Certificate of Co-partnership in the County Courthouse at Santa Rosa. Only twenty-four adult members signed this latter agreement, but at least fifty-five individuals, including children, participated in the new experiment.[13]

The new arrivals, like their precursors, sent enthusiastic letters to their midwestern friends. Iowans received envelopes filled with leaves and flowers to show how Cloverdale blossomed while Corning still shivered under snow. Fugier, left forlornly behind as one of the trustees in Iowa, wrote eagerly for information about the new countryside and confidently planned future projects.[14] The united utopians renamed their colony the Icaria Speranza Commune. In their Articles of Agreement, Icarian communists and men of the Paris Commune scientifically planned the various phases of their economy like good Saint-Simonians – agriculture, milling, mechanical arts, the founding of schools and other colonies. The agreement broadly proposed "to establish for humanity, as an example and in devotion to its welfare, a system of society capable of rendering it happy, and to prove to our fellow men that community based on solidarity is realizable and possible."[15]

To fulfill these purposes Icaria Speranza established community of property but with certain qualifications unlike earlier Icarias.

[13]The legal form of partnership was chosen over that of a corporation. The partnership is easier, does not require a lawyer to draft and submit papers, hence is cheaper, and is more truly communal because each member is responsible under the law for every other member. *Sonoma County Directory and Gazetteer* (San Francisco, 1885), p. 31, gives a brief description of the new community and its Articles of Agreement. For the Articles, see also Shaw, *Icaria*, pp. 204-16.

[14]E. Fugier to A. Marchand, Corning, Iowa, Dec. 21, 1884; letter in possession of Ernest Marchand, San Diego, Calif.

[15]Certificate of Co-partnership, County Clerk's Office, Santa Rosa. With only verbal changes the same statement appeared in the Contract and Articles of Agreement, Shaw, *Icaria*, p. 204.

The Theosophical Temple and Homestead at Point Loma, San Diego

A Group of the Icaria Speranza Commune, Cloverdale, about 1885

The community fund consisted of all money or possessions owned by the colony or by individuals before joining. At the end of each year an inventory determined the new surplus. This profit figure was then divided in two parts: the first remaining with the community as a whole, the second divided equally among the members. The division, however, was purely a bookkeeping arrangement, for the credits thus accumulated on an individual's ledger page were payable only at time of his withdrawal. Until that time the funds were used, like any other property, as community capital. The accounts further credited each individual with "labor premiums," another departure from earlier Icarian theory. Each person received a premium of one dollar and a half, one dollar, or fifty cents each month, depending on whether he had missed no days, one day, or two days from work, regardless of cause.

The profit divisions and labor premiums smacked of heresy to more orthodox socialists like Jules Leroux. But even more drastic individualism loomed in the private ownership of wardrobes, household furniture and bedding, and gifts of less than fifty dollars' value per year. Clothing, however, was distributed, if not owned, in a more truly communal system. A committee determined, with the approval of the General Assembly, the necessary annual apparel for man, woman, or child. Each individual then received his determined credit on the books of a local Cloverdale merchant. Within this budget the member could choose and plan his own outfit.

Administration of the colony differed substantially from earlier Icarian practice. In the place of individual officers stood five elected committees—Works, Home Consumption, Education, Commerce, and Accounts. Two members from each of these committees composed the Board of Administration which assumed all executive functions. In case of disagreement any question could be referred to the General Assembly, the source of all power. The assembly included all members over twenty-one, male or female, and met at least twice a year, usually far more often. A three-fourths majority settled most decisions, but certain revisions of the constitution and actions involving admission and expulsion required nine-tenths.

The provisions for the entrance of new members reflected bitter past experience. The schism of 1878 at Corning had been attributed to inadequate screening of applicants, especially of the newer French exiles following 1871. Icaria Speranza followed the Icarian pattern by admitting as novitiates only those who read and spoke French fluently, but they also required approval by nine-tenths of the General Assembly. Previous Icarias had allowed men to petition for complete membership after six months in the community; Icaria Speranza demanded a full year in the provisional status.

A new member arriving in late 1884 or early 1885 would find at first glance nothing of striking contrast with any other vineyard community of Sonoma County. No phalanstère or communal hotel interrupted the rows of vineyards. Instead, small frame dwellings clustered loosely around a two-story, white clapboard homestead with high attic and broad porches.[16] Here all members dined together and shared in social activities.

Family life was, however, not disturbed in any other way. None of the Icarian colonies ever submitted to theories of racial hygiene or genetics, in spite of Cabet's picture of marriage boards and planned parenthood in the *Voyage en Icarie*.[17] Instead, marriage was considered indispensable to man's happiness and to the stability of community life. The Icarian Constitution of 1850 even stated "the community is based on marriage and on family purified of all that alter or render them unnatural. Voluntary celibacy is interdicted; all who are enabled and disposed to marry ought to do so."[18] Icarians permitted divorce, but urged those separated to remarry speedily.

[16]Contemporary description in *Sonoma Democrat* (Santa Rosa), Mar. 20, 1886. The main house still stands.

[17]1848 ed., p. 122. See also the discussion of Cabet's racial genetics in Herman Hausheer, "Icarian Medicine," *Bulletin of the History of Medicine*, IX (May, 1941), 524-25.

[18]*Constitution of the Icarian Community, Adopted ... 1850* (Nauvoo, 1854), p. 15; in Macdonald MS., Sterling Memorial Library, Yale University, pp. 175-85.

Possibly because of the emphasis on the family and the absence of any community nurseries, educational theory was not as revolutionary nor as prominent in the life of Icaria Speranza as it had been at New Harmony, Brook Farm, Oneida, or Hopedale, and was to be later at Point Loma. All of Icaria's children received their primary education within the wooden walls of a one-room school erected late in 1881. The colony donated land to form an Icarian School District,[19] but the educational program remained a part of the county school system. The constitution of the colony guaranteed education of all children to the age of sixteen, but no specific indoctrination in Icarian principles took place in the school. A modest sum was allocated, however, for adult propaganda, at least fifty dollars each year being spent "in publishing, advertising, and circulating the business and principles of the Icaria Speranza Commune."[20]

Following one of the great traditional industries of its homeland, the French colony early set out vineyards and pressed wine. Jeune Icarie alone, after the Iowa schism, had cultivated 3,800 Concord vines which supplied thirty-six liters of wine per day, and the *Union Republican* of Corning on October 27, 1898, attributed the success of grape culture in southwestern Iowa to the Icarian influence. True to their forebears, the California colonists planted zinfandel vines within a month of their arrival![21]

But grapes were not the only crop planted. The newspaper editor of Cloverdale, after describing forty-five acres of rooted vines, recounted these other activities at the colony in December, 1882:

Besides the vineyard, one hundred acres of fair-grade wheat land is under cultivation, and at this writing it is all sown and some of the young grain is already above ground. A thrifty orchard of five acres stretches to the west from the Healdsburg road, and includes many choice varieties of trees. Some of the finest peaches we have ever tasted were produced here.... It is the intention of the proprietors

[19]*Sonoma Democrat*, Oct. 30, 1886.
[20]Articles of Agreement; Shaw, *Icaria*, p. 205.
[21]Cloverdale *Reveille*, Oct. 29, 1881.

to increase the area of the orchard as soon as possible, and they will engage extensively in the culture of French and German prunes. They intend planting nothing but the very best varieties, and hence will make a success of the business. They also propose establishing a first-class winery and distillery as soon as their production will admit of the outlay. . . .

The low hills on every side, the road winding along and almost parallel here with the curving river, the picturesque woods and the smiling vineyards, all unite in forming a panorama transcendant in its quiet, peaceful beauty. Exclusive of vineyard and grain land, there yet remains about three hundred acres of rolling hill-land, suitable for pasture, and the colonists will utilize this by entering the cattle-raising business. They thoroughly understand this class of ranching, and prefer it to wool-growing.[22]

Since the vines were important to their economy, the California group fortunately inherited a tradition which had rejected the temperance proclivities of Etienne Cabet. In the *Voyage en Icarie* Cabet had inveighed against intemperance,[23] and in the Conditions of Admission to Nauvoo smoking of tobacco, hunting, and even fishing were proscribed along with the use of alcohol. All of these restrictions became issues in the great schism which ended with Cabet's expulsion. With his demission the Icarian program was freed of any such arbitrary taboos; and fads, vegetarianism, or interdictions never afflicted Icaria Speranza.

Organized religion entered but little into the Icarian scheme. Neither atheists nor agnostics, Icarians professed true Christianity, but the forms of religion did not greatly appeal to them. The Conditions of Admission of 1854 summarized their attitude: "To adopt for their religion the True Christianity, and for their worship the practice of Fraternity."[24] The true Christianity consisted of the primal, ethical principles of brotherhood and love. Icaria did not seek to advance its ideas by political means. Most Icarians

[22]As quoted in Shaw, *Icaria*, p. 141-42. The *Pacific Sentinel* is an erroneous reference; probably the Cloverdale *Reveille* for Dec. 21, 1882.

[23]1848 ed., pp. 119-20.

[24]P. 27; in Macdonald MS., p. 171.

as naturalized citizens were enough interested in national politics to hitch up the buggy on election day for a trip to the polls. They sought no civic office, however, and never took their community ideals into the political market-place. Jules Leroux, as we have seen, frequently criticized their indifference to socialistic political activity.

The earliest Icarians in America had felt that they lived somehow beyond the scope of American law. In leaving their native land and its political and legal restrictions, they had hoped to be governed in the New World solely by their own utopian creed. "American laws . . . cannot be called upon by Icarians. For these People, between them, there are no other laws than Icarian Laws, no other Courts and no other Juges [sic] than their General Assembly, their Sovereign to all."[25] But Icaria soon faced the necessity of invoking a political entity larger than itself. During the schism of 1856, Cabet dragged the colony into the local courts, and the Nauvoo sheriff quelled several riots within the community. American justice was again required for the distribution of the Iowa properties in 1878. By this time, however, most Icarians were registered voters and proud of the fact that no concerted Icarian attempts to supersede American law had ever been made.

Though they did not actively seek to destroy it, the Icarians, nevertheless, believed they saw evils in capitalistic society in America just as they had in France. Like most utopians, they abhorred the cutthroat competition of the outside world and agreed with Emile Peron that society was sick with "dollaromania."[26] They kept abreast of the contemporary currents of social criticism, and judged _Progress and Poverty_ "the most important book on social economy which has been published in the United States."[27]

Icaria Speranza never achieved self-sufficiency. The member-

[25]Statement attributed to Cabet in MS signed by J. B. Gerard, later president of the colony, n.d., probably 1857; in possession of Mrs. Eva Bettannier Mitchell, Pasadena, Calif.

[26]Letters from Peron to Albert Shaw; in Shaw, _Icaria_, pp. 151, 164.

[27]_La Jeune Icarie_, Aug.-Sept., 1881.

ship alone could not satisfy all labor needs and was forced to import certain skilled workmen. When the season demanded a butcher, the colony sent Charles Humbert, one of its members, all the way to San Francisco to employ a German for the purpose.[28] Occasionally the General Assembly repeated the Corning pattern by renting shops in Cloverdale in order to market colony produce.

In the early days of the association following the merger in 1883, Icaria Speranza had continually assumed that the sale of the Iowa property would pay all debts and entirely clear the California lands and buildings. If all had gone smoothly, such would probably have been true. At the end of 1883 the debt in California totaled about $6,000. Jeune Icarie owned eight hundred acres of Iowa land, which if it could have been sold at an average of eight dollars an acre, exclusive of the improvements, would have liquidated the California debt. But this simple hope ignored two important factors: the Iowa colony had left obligations of its own and there was no assurance that the land would average eight dollars an acre. Plenty of western homestead land was still available, and the early Icarians had paid only $1.25 an acre in the 1850's.

Events themselves proved even more discouraging. Emile Peron and Emile Fugier, in charge of liquidation, had little difficulty in selling 160 acres of the best land and most of the horses, cattle, and pigs. But at this point they conceived of a better way to multiply the income of Icaria. Peron suddenly set off for France where he bought Norman and Percheron horses of blooded stock to form a nucleus for horse-breeding in California. The Cloverdale Icarians, waiting apprehensively for funds from Iowa and knowing nothing of the horse-breeding scheme, in 1886 sent Eugene Mourot and Paul Leroux to check on progress of the sale. As an additional complication, about the time of the committee's arrival on the Iowa scene, outside individuals who had donated

[28]Charles Humbert to Alexis Marchand, San Francisco, March 14, 1885; letter in possession of Ernest Marchand, San Diego.

money to further the ideals of the community brought suit for a share in the settlement.

During June, 1886, the case came before the county court in Corning which immediately issued injunctions against Fugier and Peron to prohibit any further transactions. After six days of testimony, long delays, and subterfuges, a decree was rendered on August 3. The court dissolved the community; appointed a receiver to sell all properties, including the imported horses; and ordered the proceeds to be dispensed in the following order: first, all debts to be paid; second, all donors to the community to be reimbursed; third, court and receiver expenses to be defrayed; and last, the eleven remaining members of Jeune Icarie to share equally the balance.[29] The amount of money which reached California through seven of the eleven individuals is not known, but it was assuredly very little. Newspapers reported some $13,000 reimbursed to non-member donors; little could have been left after that payment alone.[30] Even if money had arrived, however, by the end of 1886 it would have come too late to save Icaria Speranza.

In July, 1887, the *Revue Icarienne* of Corning reprinted an article from Alcander Longley's *Altruist* of the preceding March in which Icaria Speranza was reported dissolved. Its property had been divided among its members who had thereafter reverted to individualism. Jules Leroux had foreseen the end as early as July, 1883, when shortly before his death he wrote in *L'Etoile*, "They have nothing active, nothing living to offer to the cause of the people, the poor, the suffering. They are dead, very dead. . . . Forget them, leave them. It is for them to rejoin, not for us to wait for them." Leroux would have liked to see the Icarians join the more active urban socialist world, but after the dissolution, most of them remained near the old colony. Some of the Dehays moved into Cloverdale where they became active in the establishment of consumers' co-operatives.[31] Others remained at Icaria

[29]The eleven: Peron and his wife, Fugier and his wife, Mourot and his wife, widow James, Michel Brumme, Michel Bronner and his wife, and Louise Mourot.

[30]*Revue Icarienne* (Corning, Iowa), July-Aug., 1886.

[31]Cloverdale *Reveille*, Mar. 21, 28, Apr. 11, 25, 1896.

Speranza, no more than a group of related families pruning the sloping vineyards which had first borne for the new utopia.

More than a few conditions had conspired against the realization of their hopes. The failure of the Jeune Icarie merger to deliver them from indebtedness struck perhaps the severest blow, and certainly the unfortunate court actions involving Peron and Fugier added psychological weights. Perhaps a dynamic leader, a John Humphrey Noyes or a Robert Owen or an Etienne Cabet, could have led them through the discouragements. But after Cabet's death Icaria had at no time followed a single magnetic leader, although, of course, each family looked to its own patriarch for leadership.

Icaria Speranza suffered under one unusual handicap which made it difficult to attract fresh recruits. The stipulation that any new applicant must speak and write fluent French excluded the vast majority of prospective Americans. During Cabet's lifetime his devoted followers in France had sent a constant stream of fresh blood to Icaria, but after his death the Paris office closed and no organized help came from France thereafter. Nor could the California group count on a flow of revolutionary French exiles as had been possible following 1848 and 1871. Thus it became extremely difficult to replace any community demissions, and any man or family returning to individualism brought the Icarian ideal that much closer to defeat.

Furthermore, members of such a colony cannot so easily be kept content when economic conditions militate against fullblown community prosperity. During 1884 California averaged some fifty per cent fewer retail sales than in 1883 and a slump period followed.[32] It is probable, too, that depressed business conditions throughout the nation made land sales at Jeune Icarie more difficult. Moreover, Sonoma County grape growers at this time lost many crops from an inadequate number of wine presses, and it is possible that Icaria Speranza suffered similarly.

[32]Cross, *Labor Movement in California*, pp. 147, 151.

Looking back on the colony and its bright promise, Armand Dehay wrote:

My heart is broken that our commune is crushed like a house built on sand, I who in my enthusiasm had labored to perpetuate the work so nobly conceived by Cabet and his disciples forty years ago....[33]

He would have been pleased to read his wife's words penned in 1934, the year of her death reflecting her faith that "though many [Icarians] failed, . . . the principle stays, and in time will be perfected. That is my belief."[34]

[33]A. Dehay to A. Marchand, Cloverdale, Calif., June 4, 1888; letter in possession of Ernest Marchand, San Diego.

[34]Marie Leroux Dehay MS. relating to Pierre Leroux, 1934; in possession of Alice M. Dehay, Cloverdale.

CHAPTER 5

The Kaweah Co-operative Commonwealth

T HE government land agents in sleepy Visalia were somewhat surprised when, within the space of a few October days in 1885, over forty people filed claims on adjacent lands in the foothills, valleys, and higher forests of eastern Tulare County. The sudden onslaught aroused suspicion, as did the fact that many of these claimants listed identical addresses in San Francisco. Having been alerted along with other land offices to avoid a repetition of certain notorious timber frauds which had occurred in Humboldt County, the agents reported their concern to their superiors in Washington. And in this way began both the tangible manifestation of a socialist dream and the long, trying struggle which brought it to bitter defeat.

Burnette G. Haskell and James J. Martin, labor leaders of San Francisco who were to head a new utopian venture, called together on November 9, 1884, sixty-eight of their fellow unionists and socialists. The group was fired with the spirit of Laurence Gronlund's *Co-operative Commonwealth*, a small volume recently published, called "the first comprehensive work in English on Socialism."[1] Gronlund purported to present European Marxism "in readable English and applied to American phenomena and American conditions by a writer possessing the American bias for the practical."[2] With the doctrines of this book fresh in their

[1] W. Ellison Chalmers, "Laurence Gronlund," *DAB*. A. J. Starkweather and S. Robert Wilson, *Socialism*, also an adaptation of Marx, and containing an Introduction by Burnette Haskell, appeared in N.Y. that same year.

[2] *Co-operative Commonwealth* (Boston, 1884), p. 10.

minds, the new associates solemnly named themselves the Co-operative Land Purchase and Colonization Association of California.

Many of the sixty-eight men had previously followed Burnette Haskell in the organization of the International Workingmen's Association in San Francisco, a radical body claiming identical ideals with the First International of Marxian socialism (also known as the International Workingmen's Association). A statement of the principles of the San Francisco I.W.A. appeared on the reverse of its membership cards:

"The Proletarians have nothing to lose but their chains. They have a world to win. Let therefore the workingmen of all countries unite!" . . . Marx. To each according to his needs. From each according to his ability. No duties without rights. No rights without duties. Educate, Organize, Agitate, Unite. Our Motto: War to the Palace, Peace to the Cottage, Death to Luxurious Idleness. Our Object: The reorganization of Society independent of Priest, King, Capitalist, or Loafer. Our Principles: Every man is entitled to the full product of his own labor, and to his proportionate share of all of the natural advantages of the earth.[3]

Along with Marxism, Haskell injected anarchism into the I.W.A. He also spearheaded an abortive national drive for unity between socialist and anarchist parties in 1883, and in the plan of action which he submitted to the eastern leaders he accepted the doctrine of physical force and looked to the day "when governments will be useless."[4] He once drafted a proposal to "Seize Mint, Armories, Sub-Treasury, Custom House, Government Steamer, Alcatraz, Presidio, newspapers."[5] In 1886 he went as far as to organize a band of his I.W.A. members in a plot to dynamite the County Hall of Records in San Francisco but sty-

[3]There were three categories of membership: students, organizers, and legislators, these carrying red, white, and blue cards, respectively. This quotation is from one of the red cards; Tulare County Library, Visalia, Calif.

[4]Chester M. Destler, *American Radicalism, 1865-1901: Essays and Documents* (New London, Conn., 1946), pp. 85, 93-94.

[5]Ira B. Cross, *History of the Labor Movement in California* (Berkeley, Calif., 1935), p. 163.

mied the coup by failing himself to appear on the night appointed.[6]

Burnette G. Haskell has been characterized as "one of the most erratic and brilliant geniuses in the history of the labor movement on the Pacific Coast."[7] Born in Sierra County in 1857, he studied law at the University of California, the University of Illinois, and Oberlin and was admitted to the bar in California in 1879. He continued to practice law sporadically throughout his life, at least when more diverting pastimes were not available. When his uncle offered him the editorship of a paper called *Truth*, Haskell gladly accepted. He was acting at that time as lawyer for the Republican State Central Committee, but while on editorial missions for his new paper, he became acquainted with the trade-union movement in San Francisco and began reading the available working-class and radical literature. Within a short time he "became without doubt the best-read man in the local labor movement,"[8] and his paper, *Truth*, became the official organ for the San Francisco Trades Assembly.

Haskell was "brilliant and resourceful," gifted with enthusiasm and a vivid imagination, but he was also erratic and undependable. He remained sincere and consistent in his hopes for mankind yet he fluctuated from movement to movement like a flooded stream seeking new channels. His earliest labor-union sympathies flowed into socialistic ideas combined with freshets of anarchism; and his later attempt at co-operative settlement was succeeded, not by an espousal of violent revolution, but by the evolutionary political action of Bellamy's Nationalism, by the ritualistic mumbo-jumbo of a civic-minded organization called the Invisible Republic, and later by Populism. Nevertheless, all of these channels ran in the larger bed of hope for the perfection of man.

Haskell was not widely popular even among his close associates. One companion, after being unnecessarily baited by the lawyer and admitting himself no match for Haskell's versatile wit, called

[6]Frank Roney, *Frank Roney, Irish Rebel and California Labor Leader: An Autobiography*, ed. by Ira B. Cross (Berkeley, 1931), pp. 473-74.

[7]Cross, *Labor Movement in California*, p. 157.

[8]*Ibid.*, p. 158; for following quotation see p. 164.

him "a little, sallow, brilliant man," for whom controversies were
meat and drink.[9] Another acquaintance once described him in
verse:

> He with burning eloquence their ardor whets,
> While nervously consuming cigarettes.[10]

The desire of Haskell and his friends to create a co-operative
community sprang largely, as already mentioned, from Laurence
Gronlund's *Co-operative Commonwealth*. Although the book
did not fully outline the structure of a socialist colony, it did
offer suggestions. Gronlund's skeletal organization, a hierarchical
scheme of divisions, departments, bureaus, and sections, was modified and adopted by Kaweah.[11] From Gronlund the colonists also
borrowed their principle of office-holding: election from below
by the workers but removal from above by responsible superiors.
The concept of the labor-check was drawn from the pages of
Gronlund, and the by-laws of the colony stipulated that any
future departments of administration should be planned along
"the lines laid down in Gronlund's *Co-operative Commonwealth*."

During the organizing discussions in San Francisco, the need
for a profitable product—easily acquired, in reasonable demand,
and bringing sufficient profit to establish a colony's economic
foundations—was early appreciated. Manufacture of terra cotta
was suggested, and some plans had been made in this direction
when a message arrived from Charles Keller, a member of the
association who had recently moved to the San Joaquin Valley.

Charles F. Keller was a native of Germany who had migrated
with his parents to Pennsylvania.[12] Following service in the Civil
War, footloose and restless, he wandered west to California;

[9]Philip Winser, "Memories," (unpublished MS, Huntington Library), pp. 126-
27. Hereafter cited as Winser MS.

[10]Will Purdy, "The Saga of the Old Colony," p. 3; appended to Winser MS.

[11]For this and the following references to Gronlund, see *Co-operative Commonwealth*, pp. 137, 141, 162, 178, 179, 181-82.

[12]For details of Keller's life, see his autobiographical MS in Historical File,
Park Naturalist's Office, Sequoia National Park. The same file contains a copy
of a letter from C. F. Keller to his son, Carl, n.p., April 14, 1921, which presents
Keller's role in the timber filings. Microfilm copies in Huntington Library.

within a few years he owned a meat market in Eureka. With a ready eye for injustice, he uncovered frauds perpetrated by Humboldt County timber interests which were using individual dummies for public land entries. According to the Timberlands Act of 1878 individuals must use such land solely for their own personal gain. Keller stirred up investigations but also aroused sufficient enmity in Eureka to ruin his business and force him to sell. He went to San Francisco, where he remained long enough to meet Burnette Haskell and James J. Martin and to join their scheme for a co-operative enterprise, then moved south to Traver in the San Joaquin Valley where he opened a grocery store and established a Tulare County chapter of Haskell's I.W.A. Shortly thereafter, he read a notice that timber resources in the Sierras of eastern Tulare County had been opened for public entry. He hired a guide, stood awed in the magnificent Giant Forest stand of *Sequoia gigantea,* and elsewhere noted rich groves of fir and spruce. He immediately notified his friends in San Francisco of his find. Keller's message held forth all the potentialities desired in a site. For the foundation of a community's economy, lumber seemed as reliable as gold bullion, especially near the booming San Joaquin Valley where the need for construction material would be insatiable.

As a consequence, during October, 1885, fifty-three men of the Co-operative Land Purchase and Colonization Association journeyed from San Francisco to file claims at the Visalia land office.[13] Several of the filers could not claim American citizenship, and seven of the applicants gave the same address, a boarding house at 317 Broadway Street, San Francisco, all of which provided tinder for suspicion of illegality. The claims were classified in two categories: under the Timberland Act of 1878, and under the Homestead Act of 1862 by squatter rights. On December 2, 1885, the land office in Washington withdrew the area from entry subject to investigation, but none of the colonists con-

---

[13]The most reliable list of filings is that presented to the United States District Court, Los Angeles, by the Land Office in Visalia, included in the records of Case 278, Criminal, old series, in a sheaf labeled "Agreed Facts."

sidered the matter more than a temporary inconvenience. Since fear of fraud had instigated the withdrawal, and since, in their minds, no fraud was involved, they assumed the matter would be shortly resolved. Under this illusion the colony commenced operations, never realizing that the great shackles were already attached which would eventually bring destruction.

Surveying parties of registered engineers and of prospective colonists roamed the proposed sections. They named their colony Kaweah for the river which watered its land, and, like the stream, the colony dream was fresh and vigorous. The fabulous timber of the Giant Forest had been declared commercially inaccessible, but the Kaweahans considered themselves unbound by the rules of private enterprise. They planned to build a railroad to the foot of the hills and a road to the timber, haul the cut lumber to the valley, and float their produce down their own canals to tidewater. They envisioned within a few years their own ships at San Francisco loading the colony's own surplus: "olive oil, pure Mount Vineyard wine, honey, curly redwood veneers, statuary marble, and selected California fruits." Colonists would sail these ships to Europe, "touching at the South Sea Islands, Australia, India, Good Hope, Madeira, visiting the Mediterranean and the coast of Europe, there to discharge and reload with freight for New York and Colony via Cuba, the Brazils, Peru and Mexico, home."[14]

The vision was dazzling. In the process of establishing economic security, they would be reveling in art, music, and culture, minimizing hard labor, enjoying frequent recreation, and nurturing the lovely form of human co-operation. In this spirit Kaweah was born.

By far the colony's largest group of supporters lay in the non-resident class. These were members in a technical sense, because they paid membership fees and voted, but they never actually lived at Kaweah. San Francisco and Los Angeles had the most active groups of non-resident members, but Denver and New York City both had sizable clubs. George Hopping for many

[14]*Commonwealth* (San Francisco), II (May 24, 1889), 82.

years spirited the New York Kaweahans and proved his devotion by sending his own children, four sons and a daughter, to the colony. Unwilling, however, to abandon a good position with a firm of wholesale druggists, he did not come to the colony himself till near the end of its existence.[15] Laurence Gronlund, revered by the colony as we have seen, joined Kaweah as a non-resident member in Boston and was elected general secretary in 1890; but a voluntary fund to help him move his family from the East to California never materialized sufficiently to enable him to serve his term of office at the colony. The local clubs presented the colony from time to time with donations and gifts, which it is to be hoped, were usually more practical than the Oakland Nationalist Club's contribution of fifty rare, potted, Japanese chrysanthemums.[16]

Of Kaweah's resident members Haskell said in retrospect: "There were dress-reform cranks and phonetic spelling fanatics, word purists and vegetarians. It was a mad, mad world, and being so small its madness was the more visible."[17] Another colonist said of his comrades, "We were certainly a motley lot, assorted cranks of many creeds and none, erratic ranges from uncooked food believers to spiritualists, Swedenborgians, . . . atheists, of course, [and] a sprinkling of the orthodox."[18] On the other hand, after a visit during which he was even allowed free access to the accounts, William Carey Jones of the University of California commented: "They are all, perhaps without exception, intelligent, thoughtful, earnest, readers of books and journals, alive to the great economic and social questions of the day."[19]

The application blanks for membership support Jones's estimate. These sheets requested the stock information: name, address, citizenship, date of birth, marital status, and number in

---

[15]Winser MS., p.116.

[16]*Commonwealth* (San Francisco), III (Nov., 1889), 176.

[17]Burnette G. Haskell, "Kaweah," *Out West*, *XVII* (Sept., 1902), 315.

[18]Winser MS., p. 120.

[19]William C. Jones, "The Kaweah Experiment in Co-operation," *Quarterly Journal of Economics*, VI (Oct., 1891), 70.

Courtesy of Bancroft Library

Kaweah: CHILD OF MISFORTUNE

Part of the Kaweah Colony before the Karl Marx Tree (now more widely known as the General Sherman Tree), 1889

family. But later blanks, products of longer experience, asked the applicant to list the economic, political, or historical books he had read during the preceding year, the political organizations to which he belonged, and the labor or economic journals to which he subscribed. An early pamphlet recommended that a prospective member follow a course of preparatory reading including the works of Gronlund, Mary Howland, and A. K. Owen.[20] Kaweah clearly tried to attract thoughtful and well-read members.

Occupationally the members were largely skilled laborers from trade-unions, although some men, like George Patch from a Kansas City hay-press company, had been managers or owners of businesses. A few were artists, musicians, or literati. Many came to Kaweah dissatisfied with their status in capitalist society, and since Kaweah could not always offer desired positions, inevitable friction resulted. Haskell said that altogether about four hundred members resided at or paid extended visits to the colony at some time; but the number did not exceed 150 toward the end.[21] It probably never went higher than three hundred during any one period, and for long intervals the resident members averaged no more than fifty or seventy-five.

The Bellamy movement directed a steady stream of members to Kaweah, even from as far away as England. Philip Winser, on his farm, "Merrington," in Kent, after hearing of *Looking Backward*, procured and read the book. The eldest son of a dissenting Unitarian family, Winser had been "pondering the anomalies of society, and how it was that the hardest workers of them seemed to get the worst of it.... The answer seemed to come to me in this book...."[22] He wrote to Boston for literature concerning the Bellamy clubs and in the return pamphlets he read of the Kaweah Colony and knew he had found his utopia. He immediately applied for membership to James J. Martin, sec-

[20]"Kaweah, A Co-operative Common Wealth" (San Francisco, 1887), p. 16. Sequoia Natl. Park Historical Files.

[21]Haskell, "Kaweah," *Out West*, XVII (Sept., 1902), 317.

[22]Winser MS., p. 70.

retary at Kaweah. On receiving a favorable reply, he sold the
family farm, bought at a seaside resort a boarding house which
he gave to his mother and remaining family, fitted out a tool box,
folded under his arm the hammock he had slept in since a boy,
packed two English tweed, plus-four suits, and sailed from Liverpool. In Boston he attended a Nationalist Club meeting and met
Edward Bellamy, who shook his head over Kaweah; no such experiment, Bellamy thought, could succeed on less than a national
scale. But Winser, undaunted, crossed the continent, climbed
aboard the biweekly stage at Visalia, and arrived at the colony
on February 23, 1891, eager to prove that co-operation and
Nationalism offered practical keys to the salvation of society.

If Bellamy's work drew many a member to Kaweah, so also
did purely personal reasons. A co-operative Eden offered refuge
from a cold, competitive world. Dusty city existence would be
exchanged for clear mountain air and scenery. Kaweah, thoroughly democratic, would break all class lines, and every individual would be placed in the position for which he was best fitted.
Colony literature, like the following statement, revealed the frequently personal nature of the dream.

Here the Man shall be sunk in the State and yet shall be given such
freedom for growth and development that he, like some golden pin-
nacle of a perfect palace, shall tower far above the foundation walls.
. . . Here men shall lock their lips too close to lie, and wash their hands
too white to filch from other men. Here shall be Joy, Music, and
Laughter, Art, Science, and Beauty, and all things else for which
Poets have sung and Martyrs died, and of which in the outer world
we see but the palest phantoms.[23]

Yet Kaweah was to be more than an isolated haven in a capitalist world. It would grow into a giant yardstick against which
the proletariat could judge the superiority of communal over
capitalist systems. The plan of organization stated, "Chiefs of
departments will be organized into a board of administration,

[23]*Commonwealth* (San Francisco), III (Nov., 1889), 112.

national or other, as the case may be."[24] The Deed of Settlement added:

The general nature of the business to be transacted is to engage in the production and distribution of wealth; the collection [and] extraction of raw material ... the culture of both animal and vegetable products, ... establishment of proper methods of distribution ... credit, account and exchange ... the practice among ourselves of just systems of social organization. ... And as well *to propagate and extend in the world at large the idea of universal and just co-operation.*[25]

Kaweah's projected organization, complex, ponderous, and naive, was once described as "a locomotive's machinery on a bicycle."[26] It was based upon sound principles—responsibility to some one person for every act and ultimate appeal to the combined membership in General Meeting—but was too cumbrous for practical execution. The earliest plan, adapted from Gronlund—a massive welter of three divisions, thirteen departments, over fifty bureaus, and countless sections—soon proved too elaborate for the simple realities at the colony. In time a more modest system prevailed. This consisted of eight departments, each with a superintendent;[27] above them a Board of Trustees; and, ruling supreme, the General Meeting. The trustees, as the executive body of the company, gradually assumed powers which were never gracefully relinquished by the Meeting, and later colony history found factions at frequent loggerheads with the trustees.

[24]Jones, "Kaweah Experiment," *Quarterly Journal of Econ.*, VI (Oct., 1891), 61; italics mine.

[25]The Deed of Settlement, the basic constitution of the colony, was adopted March 7, 1888, and was frequently reprinted in colony publications thereafter. See, e.g., *A Pen Picture of the Kaweah Co-operative Colony* (San Francisco [1889]), p. 26. Italics mine.

[26]George Stewart, "History of the Kaweah Colony" (unpublished MS based on articles appearing in the Visalia *Delta* during Nov. and Dec., 1891; in Tulare Public Library, Tulare, Calif.); article of Dec. 3, 1891, p. 3. Hereafter cited as Stewart MS.

[27]The departments: Education, Growing, Transportation, Handcraft, Collection (the mill work), Public Service, Finance, Administration. B. G. Haskell to W. C. Jones, Kaweah, Aug. 28, 1891; Bancroft Library.

The General Meeting assembled the first Saturday in each month, and, since most work ceased for the occasion, it was well attended by the resident members. On rare occasions debate lasted for several days. E. G. Dudley, the blacksmith, however, refused to suspend his work for the sessions, and his vigorous hammer ringing beneath the windows of the meeting sounded his protest against the argumentation. The discussions waxed vehement. The secretary once gesticulated wildly enough to topple a jar of molasses over his minutes. The gathering of the members for the General Meeting gave rise to special festivities on those Saturday nights with music and socials and dancing in the tent-houses or the main hall.

Kaweah built its economy upon a time-check, which meant to its members: no work, no bread. The check was issued in denominations of from ten to twenty thousand minutes. All work claimed equal value; the carpenter and the trustee both received thirty cents an hour. And the time-checks provided, of course, the official medium of exchange in all intra-colony transactions. Most checks bore in the lower left corner their rate of redemption: five cents for ten minutes; $100 for twenty thousand minutes. This "crystallized labor of Kaweah,"[28] backed by the vast timber resources of the colony, would, it was thought, some-day possess value far above government notes, even in the outside world.

A membership in the colony cost $500. After an initial $100, the balance could be paid in goods or labor. Over $53,545 in cash flowed into the treasury from 1888 to 1892. For one three-year period, the colony supplied an average of sixty-five members with food, clothes, tools, and supplies at the miraculous rate of $14.50 per person per month.[29]

Such a budget provided few luxuries. For many months canvas

---

[28]Stewart MS., article of Nov. 19, 1891, p. 4.

[29]This does not include, however, the $34,278 received in the form of colony time-checks. To estimate their actual cash equivalent would be impossible. "Secretary's Statement of Receipts in Time-checks and Cash, from Inception to Jan. 1, 1892," *Commonwealth* (Kaweah, Calif.), III (Feb., 1892), 2-3.

supplied the only shelter. The tent-town of Advance housed all of the families till the end of 1889, and many of the men, especially those working on the road, lived in tents almost constantly. The main settlement of Kaweah, six miles down the canyon from Advance, gradually exhibited a few clapboard cabins. After lumber began to be carted down from the mill in the summer of 1890, a community center rose—the hall for dining and meetings, the community store, a print shop and a blacksmith shop, a barn, and some sheds. But even at Kaweah many of the bachelors slept for months in the hay of an open barn and boarded out among the families for their meals.

The colony bore all medical expenses for its members although it had no resident doctor. The most experienced matron officiated at births, but when a physician was needed, Dr. S. S. Guy, a non-resident member living nearby, was called. Outside clergymen were also required for weddings and burials. In spite of Haskell's grandiose plans for cremations at an altar on Moro Rock,[30] burials were conducted in frontier simplicity with pine boxes under colony soil. As a group Kaweah simply ignored religious organization, allowing the individual to pursue any denominational practices he saw fit.

Daily life within the colony was hard but enjoyable. At various times a band and an orchestra were rehearsing, and their evening concerts under summer stars, though interrupted by the howling of the coyotes, were appreciated not only by the colonists but by outsiders who drove up in buggies from the valley. Literary and scientific classes were occasionally held. A home circle gathered on Saturday nights to discuss problems of marriage and the family. Dances were occasionally given, although they faced opposition from those who held dancing to be a sin. Even George Stewart, newspaperman of Visalia and an open critic of Kaweah, admitted that "there was much talent and hope. Lectures, readings, and excellent music were enjoyed by the colonists and listened to and participated in with genuine pleasure and profit."[31]

[30]*Commonwealth* (San Francisco), III (Nov., 1889), 125.
[31]Stewart MS., article of Nov. 19, 1891, p. 4.

Picnics provided a frequent recreation. Overnight trips were made into the Giant Forest area where picnickers and campers often took snapshots of the redwoods. The colonists named the larger sequoias after socialist thinkers or heroes; the tree they called the Karl Marx is now more widely known as the General Sherman. Closer to home the river afforded good swimming during hot summer days. The editor of an eastern journal, hearing of the spring chicken and buttermilk parties, the strawberry and blackberry pickings, the haying and the mountain climbing, extolled, "Kaweah! embryonic regenerator of the sphere; Kaweah! where life is every day a picnic!"[32]

Kaweah's first and principal effort was bent toward the building of its road, which in all the colony's literature stands as a symbol of future glory. Though timber interests had dismissed the redwood area as inaccessible, Kaweah maintained that the power of co-operation would make light the obstacles. The actual shoveling began early in October, 1886, with Andrew Larsen, a wiry Norwegian ship-captain, Horace Taylor, the most efficient and skilled of Kaweah's general managers, Thomas Markusen, Martin Schneider, and Charles F. Keller at the spades. Mrs. Taylor and Mrs. Keller cooked for this first work camp. For four slow years the road painstakingly took shape, its work often being pushed to the exclusion of more immediate tasks such as the planting of crops or orchards. Much of the course, picked and shoveled by hand, ascended precipitous granite ledges, and dynamite had to be used sparingly because of its expense. Before completion, the route attained an altitude of 8,000 feet on a steady grade of eight feet to the hundred for a distance of eighteen miles. It reached the pines in June, 1890, four years after it was begun.

When Haskell called the road a "stupendous work,"[33] he in no way exaggerated. Long after the area became Sequoia National Park, the route remained the only entrance into the Giant Forest. A modern highway has since been built, but the old road can still

[32]*Twentieth Century*, July 3, 1890; as reprinted in *Commonwealth* (Kaweah), I (Aug. 9, 1890), 2.
[33]"Kaweah," *Out West*, XVII (Sept., 1902), 316.

be traveled, with permission from the Ranger Service, from Kaweah to Old Colony Mill.

Kaweah fondly hoped that a high type of education could be provided for young and old. The Deed of Settlement promised "education of ourselves and our children in proper physical, mental, moral, intellectual, and artistic lines."[34] An indication of achievement in the physical sphere was the extensive collection of sporting equipment—Indian clubs, horizontal and parallel bars, rings, exercise machines, boxing gloves, baseball bats and uniforms, fencing foils—inventoried in 1891 by the Bureau of Physical Culture of the Department of Education. A kindergarten and a primary school held regular sessions, but the schoolhouse could not boast a floor till the spring of 1889. Pupils called their teachers by their first names and were spared any sort of corporal punishment. Lack of discipline, however, resulted not so much from absence of physical punishment as from the political organization in which a child could threaten the teacher with dismissal through his father at the next General Meeting. Since some unconscious antagonism against the "soft job" of teaching lurked in the minds of the workers, the General Meeting on several occasions did transfer a teacher from the school to another position. Such a possibility often placed the whip in the hand of the pupil.

Nevertheless, a high degree of general intellectual life was achieved. Some adult classes met. The *Commonwealth* often carried more articles of a broad, thoughtful nature than it did news accounts and reflected a genuine interest in contemporary thinking. For example, the issue of March 1, 1890, included an essay of Robert Ingersoll on the evils of a loveless marriage, accounts of the French communal village at Guise, descriptions of the immutable laws which govern social and industrial relations, and reports of unscrupulous exploitation and the problems of the working man. Members heatedly discussed current events in their daily contacts as well as at meetings of the Nationalist Club, which provided one of the most active intellectual outlets at the colony.

[34] "Deed of Settlement," in *A Pen Picture of the Kaweah Co-operative Colony*, (San Francisco, [1889]), p. 26.

The club met every Wednesday night in a specially designated
tent that also housed the organization's library.

Unfortunately debates were not always of a dispassionate nature; often they reflected the internal squabbles which continually sapped the constructive strength of the colony. The first of
the great disputes came in the last months of 1887 and concerned
definitions of the colony as a legal entity. Up to this time Kaweah
had been simply a "voluntary association" with no legal status. In
order to convey lands to the colony it became necessary to form
either a joint stock company, in which the shares would be trans-
ferable without the consent of the total body, or a corporation, in
which more rigid control of the shares was possible. Keller led a
bitter fight for the latter against Haskell and the majority of the
members, who maintained that the fluidity of a joint stock company tended to minimize the danger of control by a few and
allowed greater democratic administration. When the matter came
to final decision and the Haskell element won, some fifty members
withdrew from the colony and issued a formal protest. These
malcontents, most of whom later lived in San Francisco, named
themselves the Democratic Element. From time to time during the
following years they published innuendoes and outright charges
against Kaweah, speaking of themselves as former, disillusioned
members. But schism or no, Kaweah was henceforth designated
"The Kaweah Co-operative Commonwealth Company of California, Ltd., A Joint Stock Company."

Another major disagreement erupted in the winter of 1889. It
centered around the publication of a complete list of non-resident
members and their addresses, which Haskell consistently refused,
on the ground that open publication would unfairly expose individuals to the charge of socialism. But various residents looked
upon the reluctance as an attempt to conceal illicit activities, and
the charges waxed strong. The Democratic Element in San Francisco claimed that the trustees were withholding the lists so that
a general referendum of all members could not be called. The
trustees countercharged that the whole affair was stirred up by
agents paid to wreck the colony and that the circular letters of

the Democratic Element were forgeries. So the accusations flew and the colony was using vital energy in futile, nonproductive disputes.

Aside from the larger factional divisions, squabbles between individuals seemed incessant. Mr. Freeze, colony watchmaker, sold Martin a watch for ninety dollars in time-checks. Some time later when Freeze had left the colony, he demanded the return of the watch, saying it had been purchased with bogus money. The courts upheld Freeze, and Martin was forced to surrender the watch. Some members frequently charged the others with laziness and parasitic existence. Haskell remembered seeing a woman cutting wood with an ax and bucksaw in plain view of thirteen men gathered for six hours around a stump arguing a rule of order which had been misconstrued at the last General Meeting. Furthermore, the occupationally misplaced complained. An accomplished landscape artist worked for months at the wash-tub, and a graduate of three conservatories of music spent days cooking in the restaurant. "These little pin pricks ... killed the noble purpose and enthusiasm of the enterprise and slowly drained its life away."[35]

More than a pin prick, however, was Haskell's own personality —argumentative and undependable. As early as 1888 James Martin, general secretary and long-time friend of Haskell, wrote to him angrily that his failure to be prompt with replies from San Francisco was causing great inconvenience and confusion. At another time he labeled Haskell "unfriendly, uncomradelike and unbusinesslike." "It seems to me that you *delight* in trying my patience by keeping me in needless suspense. ... For God's sake be *prompt*."[36] By 1891 the personality conflict between these two men had broken into open rupture. Most of the remaining members sided with Martin, and Haskell isolated himself like a snarling dog in his cabin at the colony.

As a matter of fact, all of the Kaweah leadership was inexperienced and made frequent mistakes. Provision should have been

[35]Haskell, "Kaweah," *Out West*, XVII (Sept. 1902), 318.
[36]Martin to Haskell, April 23, 1888, and June 4, 1889; Bancroft Library.

made for a fuller screening of prospective members to insure the colony against the inclusion of those who had little appreciation of the meaning of co-operation. The leaders also might wisely have directed more serious efforts toward agricultural production rather than conducting such a large proportion of energy into the building of the road. Furthermore, the trustees erred greatly in assuming that the land-claims problem would eventually be decided in their favor. They allowed new members to believe the land titles were not seriously endangered. In answer to a direct question from a prospective colonist, "whether the colony has a good title to the lands," Haskell responded, ". . . if we have been satisfied to expend nearly a hundred thousand dollars in improvements, you need hardly fear for your small amount. It is impracticable and unnecessary to explain the details of our title to the public."[37] Certainly after four years of governmental indecision, the trustees should have given some thought to possible alternatives, and tentative plans for removal to a different site should have been made.

Yet in spite of its internal troubles, Kaweah might conceivably have succeeded had it not been for the external hostility which made its inward maladies lethal. It is possible that all of the unfriendliness on the part of the federal government, the courts, and the press was the surface expression of more basic antagonisms. The timber interests of California had sufficient cause to fear the competition of a group about to exploit the rich sequoia area, and it is perhaps more than coincidental that the most violent attacks did not open until the colony's road into the timber neared completion. Martin was convinced that the local Republican clubs were working secretly against the colony, and certainly the Kaweah members fervently believed that the hostility sprang from vested interests.[38]

The United States government was the first to reflect animos-

[37]*Commonwealth* (San Francisco), II (May, 1889), 83.

[38]*Commonwealth,* Dec. 8, 1890; Haskell, "Kaweah," *Out West,* XVII (Sept., 1902), 317; Visalia *Times-Delta,* Sept. 25, 1930; Jones, "Kaweah Experiment," *Quarterly Journal of Econ.,* VI (Oct., 1891), 69; Winser MS., p. 130.

ity. Shortly after the Kaweah claims were filed, as we have seen, the area was withdrawn from entry and the existing petitions suspended for further investigation. The suspicions of the land agents were intensified by rumors that the Southern Pacific Railroad lurked behind the colonists. The Kaweah members themselves considered the tales so absurd that they were confident the lands would be speedily reopened following inquiry. Meantime, under advice from the land office, they "squatted" while the co-operative venture began.

Certain important conclusions emerged in the long and complex story of the land claims. Government decisions on the matter of the title were not forthcoming even four years after the original filings. Such laxity seems inexcusable. It is true that each applicant for timberland swore that he had not made any agreement "by which the title he may acquire from the government of the United States shall inure in whole or in part to the benefit of any person except himself."[39] Individual colonists planned to assign their perfected titles to the Kaweah Co-operative Colony, Inc., and in this sense it may be construed that they intended to break the law. On the other hand, the same Act of 1878 made specific provisions for associations of persons. A special agent of the Government Land Office, B. F. Allen, stated in a report to his superiors: "I can say without hesitation that I have never seen a case of timber entry where the spirit and intention of the land laws were being carried out in better faith."[40] On September 25, 1890, Congress established the Sequoia National Park and a few days later set apart the adjacent lands as a national forest. After four years of procrastination, the land office was now relieved of the necessity of decision, and the colonists had but one remaining course: to seek reimbursement for the lands and improvements. The government denied the necessity of such payment because the colony had never held full legal title and the improvements were

[39]Timberlands Act of 1878, reprinted as Doc. No. 18, U. S. General Land Office, Circular . . . Showing the Manner of Proceeding to Obtain Title to Public Lands (Washington, D.C., 1892), p. 147.

[40]Congressional Record, 52d Congress, 2d Session, XXIV, Part II, 1471.

made after the land was withdrawn from entry. The government's position was logical and legal, but it was not just. A Congressional investigation in 1893 of the Kaweah claims for payment produced a report favorable to the colonists,[41] but no governmental action ever resulted.

No one can deny the vital importance of preserving for posterity the redwoods of the Giant Forest, but Kaweah might never have cut them even if it had obtained title to the land. As J. J. Martin said: "The colonists were sufficiently visionary and intelligent to perceive that these giant trees would be worth a thousand times more to them standing, as objects of scientific interest and public attraction, than they would be were they cut into lumber."[42] Personal pledges of a few individuals would not, however, have been sufficient safeguard against destruction. But, regardless of the necessity, the governmental handling of the Kaweah land claims must be censured. William Carey Jones, whose comments on the members have already been noted and whose later position as Director of the Law School of the University of California entitles him to some attention, summarized: "In the matter of the controversy with the government, I can come to no other conclusion than that a great injustice has been done to those persons who in good faith made filings for timber claims in October, 1885. . . . The law of the case is not so clear to my mind. It is difficult to find consistency in the decisions of the Land Office. . . . But even the law seems to me to incline in favor of the timberland claimants."[43]

Outside of socialist and labor organs, Kaweah never knew the warmth of sympathetic news reporting. Beginning around 1890, the editors of California took delight in printing black or ludicrous accounts of the colony's last fumbling efforts. Haskell referred to the press as stabbing Kaweah to death.[44] The San Francisco *Chronicle* used such innuendo as that in an article of December

[41]*Senate Reports*, 52d Congress, 2d Session, I, No. 1248.
[42]J. J. Martin to the Editor of the Fresno *Bee*, July 17, 1928.
[43]Jones, "Kaweah Experiment," *Quarterly Journal of Econ.*, VI (Oct., 1891), 72.
[44]"Kaweah," *Out West*, XVII (Sept., 1902), 316.

8, 1891: "... it would be interesting to know what has happened to the rest of the money." The same journal on December 1, 1889, had described the colonists as "miserable people," "deluded beings," "imposed on by unscrupulous men." The San Francisco *Star* on April 20, 1890, carried editorials calling Kaweah a "villainous gang" and a "practical despotism," as a result of which six days later the *Pacific Union*, a labor paper, printed signed statements from all the residents of Kaweah denying completely the *Star's* "vicious statements." The Visalia *Times-Delta* on September 25, 1890, accused the Kaweah people of being "sent into the park area as the unwitting tools of the lumber barons." The Fresno *Daily Republican* on November 22, 1891, called the colony "an infamous bunco game" and continued: "For from five to seven years this pair of scheming plotters [i.e., Haskell and Martin] have been deluding individuals into sending money and eventually going themselves and taking their families into this mountain trap. . . ." This same account pictured the colonists gathering small bags of weeds as their only current food.

Further evidence of external hostility toward Kaweah is found in criminal case 201 in the records of the United States District Court at Los Angeles. On January 2, 1891, the Kaweah trustees were charged with the unlawful cutting of five pine trees growing on public land to the value of two dollars each. These trees were cut during the earliest of the lumber operations when the road to the timber had barely been completed. The trustees notified the workers not to log beyond a given point, but in the enthusiasm of the first actual lumbering, the men overstepped the line by five trees. Certain of the trustees soon thereafter noticed the mistake and severely reprimanded the miscreants; but the trees had been felled. The court in Los Angeles, after some litigation, found the defendants guilty and fined them from $100 to $300 apiece. Even Stewart, hostile critic that he was, said of the first trial: "In this instance the timber-cutting was not done with evil intent, and it would seem that notice to desist should have been sufficient."[45]

[45]Stewart MS., article of Dec. 24, 1891.

The second important trial, criminal case 278 in the same court, points even more strikingly to the existence of hostile elements outside of the colony. In an indictment filed January 9, 1892, the government charged the trustees with illegal use of the mail in furtherance of a scheme to defraud. The practice in question concerned mailing propaganda and receiving donations. In this case Judge Erskine M. Ross instructed the jury to acquit on the grounds of insufficient evidence. Ross, who before his position in the federal judiciary had served for seven years on the California Supreme Court, stated that the accounts of the colony showed a most marvelous economy, an honest administration, and a devotion and self-sacrifice unexampled in business affairs.[46]

Reviewing the whole process, Haskell caustically remarked:

The capitalist press used their banal reporter's English to stab us to death; the lumber monopoly of the San Joaquin went to Congress behind our back and made a "Park" of the Forest we had saved from flame. The machinery of the law was used to take us three hundred miles to meet charges in court without one single jot of evidence, while gigantic lumber thieves were looting the forests of Humboldt and the authorities winked their eye. We were poor. We were ignorant. We were jeered at. But no man dare say but we were honest.[47]

Kaweah's last days—a slow disintegration marked by no single act of finality—held bitter memories. A reduced number of colonists lived on the few acres remaining after the Congressional actions of 1890. Donations and fees from non-residents had fallen to a mere trickle. William Christie, long-time trustee, offered Visalia merchants five hundred dollars worth of time-checks for ten dollars in cash. One sensitive colonist, who had planned to bring his prospective bride to a new home at Kaweah, shot himself in despondency partly, at least, over the colony's imminent failure. In November, 1891, about half of the resident members abolished the time-checks, took possession of the land and ma-

---

[46]Francis J. McClary, Affidavit of F. J. McClary in Regard Kaweah Colony (a notarized copy of the statements of Dist. Atty. Allen, for the prosecution; H. C. Dillon for the defense; and Judge Ross for the court), Feb. 16, 1893.

[47]Haskell, "Kaweah," Out West, XVII (Sept., 1902), 316-17.

chinery, and repudiated the debts of the old workers. But this act only symbolized, in Haskell's phrase, "coyotes quarreling over a carcass."[48]

During the month that preceded the trial of 1892, Haskell spent his time at Kaweah, isolated and discredited, watching the families packing, moving, or disputing disposition of the goods. On April 7 he wrote in his diary: "The motto on my mantelpiece reads, 'I owe much. I have nothing. I give the rest to the poor.' That about states my case."[49] Waiting impatiently for the trial, and spending the days prospecting in the hills, he had picked up several specimens with "gold stains." Hope ran high, and he entered a revealing passage in his diary.

After careful thought I have solemnly determined if any mine is discovered and I make a fortune out of it that I will use that fortune in order to practically make human beings better. This can be done by education; by assisting state control; by the establishing of prize funds for valor, perseverence, fidelity, etc.; by building up a labor farm; especially by checking corruption through making the attorneys paid officers of the state. . . . Justice is not free, nor is it half the time secured when paid for. . . . With justice to be had, morals would improve. I will so use my fortune if I get it.

Through bitterness and hardship Haskell remained an idealist. Three days later, on April 15, the idealist discovered that the brass nails on his boots had scratched the "gold stains" on the rock surfaces. On that date he entered in the diary, "hugely disgusted."

Haskell had helped his wife plant a few poor vegetables, and on April 18 he recorded: "The pigs ate up all the potatoes on the flat today; also the squash. Oh, Hell!"

Yet with his dream still alive, he published these histrionic passages ten years after the dissolution:

---

[48]*Ibid.*, p. 322.

[49]Haskell, B. G., and others, "A Family Record of the Haskell Tribe" (Unpublished MS, n.d.), p. 137; Bancroft Library. The subsequent quotations from this diary are on pp. 139-40, 141.

[Kaweah] was one of the hopes of my life. And seeing it now, lying dead before me, knowing that its own hands assisted in strangling it, knowing that the guilt of its death rests upon nearly all of its members, myself far from being excepted, the faltering steel that cuts the epitaph chisels as well "peccavi."

We were not fit to survive, and we died. But there is no bribe money in our pockets; and beaten and ragged as we are, we are not ashamed.

And is there no remedy, then, for the evils that oppress the poor? And is there no surety that the day is coming when justice and right shall reign on earth? I do not know; but I believe, and I hope, and I trust.[50]

[50]Haskell, "Kaweah," *Out West*, XVII (Sept., 1902), 300, 303, 322.

CHAPTER 6

Altruria

———❖———

G RAPES ripened and leaves yellowed under the clear skies of a Sonoma Valley October in 1894 as a caval-cade of buggies crossed the wooden bridge by the old mill on Mark West Creek. Eighteen adults and eight children scrambled down under the oak trees and poured through the house before which they had stopped. The women directed the excitement into work, sweeping, dusting, scrubbing. Before dark a number of wagons arrived from Santa Rosa with furniture and household goods and even a hen with seven chicks. Men stretched linen on the beds, women cooked supper, a fire crackled on the hearth. Gaiety, wit, and hope enlivened the first day of Altruria on earth.

These were Altrurians, a utopian group which had been organized in the neighborhood of San Francisco Bay. They had found their name in William Dean Howells' novel *A Traveler from Altruria* and recognized in Howells' "splendid dream" their own guiding ideal, "that of an ordered and balanced adjustment of interests, in which each individual shall have place and part and privilege, but shall at the same time hold sacred the part, the place, the privilege, of every other."[1]

Howells in his novel drew a Mr. Homos of Altruria, a traveler from utopia, who visited an exclusive New England summer hotel on his first trip to America. Mr. Homos astounded the guests by helping baggageman, waitress, and bootblack with their tasks and confounded a learned group of conversationalists on the hotel porch with embarrassing questions on American life. In the concluding chapters Homos described briefly the ideal society of

———

[1]*Altrurian,* Oct. 6, 1894.

101

his homeland, which, although not a comprehensive description of utopian life such as that found in Cabet's *Voyage en Icarie,* nevertheless inspired the California group.

The Altrurian Colony was not only an extension of Howells' ideas but, more basically, a product of Christian thought. A young Berkeley minister, Edward Biron Payne, bridged the gap between Christian ethics and Altrurian socialism. Payne, a thirty-year-old Congregationalist minister fresh from his graduation at Oberlin, arrived in Berkeley in 1875. He had been called to minister to the state university which only seven years before had opened its gates on the Berkeley hills. His father before him had been a Congregationalist minister, settling for a time in Vermont, where Edward was born in the 1840's. But somewhere in Payne's early training, perhaps in the public schools of Connecticut and Illinois, perhaps in his years of night work with Dwight L. Moody in the Chicago slums, perhaps as pastor of a village church while supporting himself and his wife during his last years at Oberlin, dissatisfaction with Congregationalist theology penetrated his thought. For five years he ministered to the Congregationalists of Berkeley and the university, but during this time he studied and pondered other systems, and on a Sunday morning in 1880 in a special message to his congregation he resigned his pastorship. Abandoning his sect as well as his congregation, he moved into the shelter of Unitarianism, along a path which the fiery Minot J. Savage had trod seven years earlier.

Like Savage, Payne rose quickly in Unitarian circles. He held pastorships in Massachusetts and New Hampshire; but in his zeal to serve the laboring class, a zeal which had led him voluntarily to churches at Manchester and Leominster, he undermined his own health and tuberculosis set in. He therefore welcomed the opportunity to return to the milder climate of Berkeley, this time as a Unitarian. California did not mean isolation for Payne; his continued high position in Unitarian circles may be judged from his inclusion on a national committee to revise the constitution of the Unitarian National Conference in 1894. Besides Payne, the committee numbered such venerable leaders as Edward Everett

Hale, Minot J. Savage, George William Curtis, John White Chadwick, and Charles Carroll Everett.[2]

Payne arrived for the second time in Berkeley as the first Unitarian minister in that town. He became a popular pastor, raising a congregation of over 150 within two years. According to William Carey Jones, professor at the university, "If Dr. Payne spoke no word but just stood before us during the service hour, we would all be flooded by the benediction of his spirit."[3] Payne vigorously and forthrightly espoused a social gospel, which was gradually leading him into Christian Socialism. Although he never had direct relationships with William D. P. Bliss's Society of Christian Socialists, reaching at this time its zenith of popularity in the East, his ideals were closely akin to those of Bliss's group. Payne advertised the *Dawn,* the Christian Socialist journal, in the *Altrurian,* the colony newspaper, and agreed with Bliss that "the teachings of Jesus Christ lead directly to some specific form or forms of Socialism."[4]

Christian Socialism disturbed the pulpits of San Francisco as it did other parts of the country during the 1890's.[5] A predominantly anti-theological movement, it stressed the immanence, not the transcendence of God and the prerequisite importance of saving society before saving the individual. From Puritanism it inherited a Calvinistic zeal for transforming this world into the Kingdom of God on earth. On the other hand, it retained from Enlightenment thought an optimistic estimate of human nature.

[2]Berkeley *Herald,* Sept. 25, 1895. George W. Cooke, *Unitarianism in America* (Boston, 1902), p. 229.

[3]Quoted in Ninetta E. Payne's Preface to Edward B. Payne, *The Soul of Jack London* (Kingsport, Tenn., 1933), p. vi.

[4]From the principles of the Society of Christian Socialists adopted in Boston, 1889, as printed in W. D. P. Bliss, ed., *New Encyclopedia of Social Reform* (N.Y., 1908), p. 203; first published as *Encyclopedia of Social Reform* (N.Y., 1897).

[5]Ralph H. Gabriel, *The Course of American Democratic Thought* (N.Y., 1940), pp. 315-21; Charles H. Hopkins, *The Rise of the Social Gospel in American Protestantism: 1865-1915* (New Haven, 1940), pp. 171-83. For the following statement on Christian Socialism I am particularly indebted to James Dombrowski, *Early Days of Christian Socialism in America* (N.Y., 1936).

It differed seriously from Marxism in seeking good will and brotherhood among all classes and in opposing rebellion or revolt. It was a socialism which stressed gradual change, interdependence and mutual obligation among men with little emphasis on the economic reform of existing society.

In San Francisco during the mid-nineties, George D. Herron, one of the most economically conscious of the Christian Socialists, addressed his radical message to overflowing audiences. His following was large enough to cause the trustees of the First Congregational Church to note with alarm the deplorable fact "that numbers of evangelical pastors welcome the unbridled socialism of Professor Herron and hail him as a prophet inspired of God."[6] Nor were the trustees any happier when Laurence Gronlund, author of the first American adaptation of Marx, whose work we have already noted as a significant factor in the founding of Kaweah, lectured enthusiastically to religious meetings and numerous church congregations. Undoubtedly Payne attended many of these gatherings and wholeheartedly endorsed their conclusions.

As a consequence of similar meetings and growing out of this milieu, a group of friends gathered around Payne and in the course of their conversations hatched a plan for a co-operative colony. It was a small group, some six or seven families and half a dozen bachelors.[7] Many of them were members of Payne's congregation; at least one was a professor from the university; most were middle-class artisans—carpenters, brickmasons, weavers, bakers. Early in 1894 they drafted a constitution, based on democratic suffrage, complete equality of community goods, but individual ownership of all possessions purchased with colony labor-checks. The officers were to serve with no limitations on length of term. Each, however, was subject to the Imperative

---

[6]*Altrurian*, May 20, 1895.

[7]The group chose the following officers in 1894: E. B. Payne, pres.; Allen V. Morse, secy.; Mrs. L. J. Watkins (supplanted in Dec., 1894, by Mrs. A. F. Aitken), vice-pres.; Mrs. Emma Woodruff, treas. The executive committee included Payne, C. S. Preble, F. E. Nelson, A. V. Morse, and B. Woodruff.

Mandate, a form of initiative in which one half of the membership could at any time demand a new election. The Executive Committee, composed of all officers, was to meet each Monday at ten in the morning to administer all affairs in the interim between meetings of the Grand Council.

In the spring of 1894 the Berkeley group appointed a committee to select a location for the colony, but the prerequisite conditions were not readily found: accessible transportation, nearness to a large city, water power, arable land, beauty, low cost. After weeks of searching, the hopefuls agreed upon a canyon just north of Fountain Grove, 185 acres of rich, wooded land along Mark West Creek, six or seven miles from Santa Rosa. Some of the steep hillsides could be used only for orchards, hay, or pasturage, but twenty-five level acres were already cultivated as a market garden. Existing evidence does not indicate the amount which the colonists paid for their land, but even at fifty dollars an acre, the price paid by Thomas Lake Harris for similar land only a few miles distant and twenty years earlier, the property would have cost over $9,000.

The initial cash for the purchase derived basically from a fifty-dollar entrance fee, which from the first eighteen adults amounted to about $900. Small sums accrued in gifts and dues from the local Altrurian clubs, but the only sizable additions to the initial fund came from members who sold their worldly belongings and donated the money to the colony. Morrison Swift, a close associate of and frequent visitor to the colony, indicated that at least some members brought in several thousand dollars apiece.[8] The economic status of the colonists was not high; on the contrary, they were families of moderate means. But some owned homes or a bit of land and, although not required to do so, often turned over their holdings to the colony.

The land and the surroundings aroused the most extravagant hopes. The *Altrurian* joyfully described a coal deposit which

[8]"Altruria in California," *Overland Monthly*, XXIX (June, 1897), 644. Two individuals, for example, offered lots in southern California and Berkeley; *Altrurian*, Oct. 25, 1894.

would provide fuel for cooking and heating, a coal of marketable quality, and the basis for large-scale industry. A quarry
of abrasive dust was to furnish Altru-Aluminum Polish, an
all-purpose burnisher which would drive Sapolio, the most
heavily advertised cleanser of the day, from the market. Such
industrial pursuits would be based on water power from Mark
West Creek, which, over a dam, could generate at least one
hundred horsepower. The lake so created would enhance the
attractive landscape, and tourists, flocking thither, would support
a large hotel with porches overlooking arbored walks winding
toward the rippling water. On such an economic foundation, the
Altrurians hoped "to make social life strong, beautiful and sweet,
and individual experience free, joyous and noble."[9] When a cor-
respondent signed a letter to the paper "Yours for Heaven now,"
the editor understandably commented, "That expression touches
our central idea."[10]

When the Altrurians drove their buggies from Santa Rosa to
their utopia in October of 1894, three houses and a grist mill stood
spaced about the level central area. During the first few nights,
three families and the bachelors slept in the mill, though the leak-
ing roof, the barrels and bales, the antiquated machinery, and
the hastily assembled carpenter shop made living difficult. "The
Mill on the Floss" grew less crowded but remained intact throughout the colony's existence. The antique machinery ground corn
and barley, and the unmarried men roomed in its loft, which
served also for office and storage space. Meanwhile the community busily constructed small cabins, scattered among its hills and
trees. By April of 1895 at least seven cottages had risen, most of
them housing individual families, although the Nelson and Par-
sons families shared a house and Grandpa Morse roomed with
bachelor Sawin. Payne himself never kept full-time residence at
the colony. He served as president from the beginning, spent long
periods there, and often stayed overnight; but he retained his

[9]E. B. Payne, "Altruria," *Amer. Mag. of Civics*, VI (Feb., 1895), 169.

[10]*Altrurian*, Nov. 22, 1894.

position in the Berkeley Unitarian church and so was required to spend much of the time in town.

The most ambitious, and in some ways most unfortunate, community project was the hotel. On February 4, 1895, the *Altrurian* proudly heralded the laying of a cornerstone for a building to answer all the social needs of the community. Located on a high bank of the creek, the hotel was planned with two stories containing seven family apartments, a dining hall, office, library, and guest rooms. The kitchen was to stretch outward as a wing and was to include living quarters on its second story. In rustic style with eaves and gables overhanging widely, the design was drawn gratuitously by an architect at the university. The colonists hoped to occupy the building in May, but in March the council decided to impose a third story on the incomplete structure, thus further delaying completion.

Although the kitchen and dining room functioned according to schedule in May, the hotel never was finished. The exposed studs and joists jutted above the little colony for most of its existence, absorbed energy and capital like the great hall at Brook Farm, and symbolized dreams unattained.

The first death preceded the first birth in the colony. The small son of Mr. and Mrs. Robert Nelson died of pneumonia within a month of the first arrivals. Frederick De Jorndt, who with his wife and children had journeyed from Florida to help charter Altruria, fashioned a casket of wood which he had brought from the Everglades. Two months later, in January, the first Altrurian child was born to one of the founding families, the Parsonses, but she lived less than a week.

Such saddening experiences served more as cementing agents than discouragements, for the winter of 1894-95 marked the height of Altrurian hope, enthusiasm, and solid co-operative accomplishment. Daily life was full and exciting. Fred Davidson, formerly of the Navy, bugled the colony to meals and assemblies. Saturday-evening socials featured recitations and song recitals and refreshments. At Christmas, presents and games around a tree on the upper floor of the old mill followed an elaborate

turkey feast. New Year's Eve provoked special merriment. Fire-
side meetings livened the middle of most weeks, while Sundays
were especially sociable with morning gatherings under the trees
for Bible readings or lectures, with picnics, mountain climbs, and
sometimes with song fests or story sessions during the evenings.
During spring and summer, in the absence of a completed hotel,
tents accommodated the week-end guests who drove up from
San Francisco or even from as far away as Los Angeles.

If Altruria had had the opportunity, it would have endowed
its children with a highly notable education. The colony planned
small school cottages, easily ventilated, flooded with light, and
surrounded with forest trees. The interiors were to cultivate the
imagination and heart of the child. He should learn "the ribs of
the mountains, feel the pulses of the sea, trace the foot paths of
the stars, summon horses and chariots of fire to make them bear-
ers of thought, set in order the secrets of the soil—make God
transitive through nature into life."[11] But the community fell as
short of its educational as of its industrial ideal. The eight to
twelve school-age children were taught by Miss Whittier from
Pasadena who was admittedly deficient compared with the colony's ideal teacher: a combination of St. Cecilia, Raphael, Crom-
well, and Job.[12]

The *Altrurian*, the colony weekly, published two issues in
Berkeley before it moved its presses to the colony. Beginning
as a four-page journal, it soon expanded to eight, printing not
only Altrurian news but attempting to cover all like-minded
groups throughout the state and country. It followed the progress
of its contemporary co-operative experiments such as Topolobampo in Mexico, Fairhope in Alabama, and an Australian settlement in Paraguay, quoted John Ruskin and Henry Demarest
Lloyd, and trained its light frequently on Eugene Debs. It
discussed and quoted ministers who had turned to Christian
Socialism, and accordingly reported in detail the California speak-

[11]*Altrurian*, Dec. 10, 1894.
[12]*Ibid.*, May 6, 1895.

ing tour of George D. Herron in 1895. A large number of its articles were by Payne himself who, as editor, wrote a sizable proportion of its material.

No reader of the *Altrurian* can fail to note the multiplicity of occupations which the colony pursued. Almost every issue reported formation of a new department and asked for orders from outsiders. Weavers offered small fancy cottons and woolens, the smithy and woodworking shops sought wider markets, a bamboo department fashioned bamboo screens and furniture, the art department constructed rustic chairs and easels, women wove jute and cotton carpets, the print shop exported job printing—all in addition to the regular domestic tasks of the poultry yard, vegetable and fruit gardens, apiary, and cattle herd. The economic emphasis was on diversification rather than co-ordination.

Members served in whatever department they desired and during whatever hours the spirit moved them. A genuine co-operative enthusiasm in men and women who joked and made fun of menial jobs overcame for awhile the problems of dispersal and continuity. No money exchanged hands, but members received colony checks in return for their labor. These checks could be used for commodities at the community store and all purchases so made became private property. Such holdings, however, could not be sold or exchanged. From their labor-checks members paid a minimum sum for rent and board.

Apparently the founders believed the fifty-dollar initiation fee and the community's cumulative production would supply sufficient capital without expropriation of individual possessions. The colony, however, came to regret its lax position on the matter of individual holdings outside the co-operative body. When a subscriber asked how many members were ready to turn over all their property and burn their bridges behind them, the editor answered, "This is what we ought all to do. It would establish us at once in such a way as to make our work a noble success."[13] "What we ought all to do" became law after a reorganization

[13]*Altrurian*, Dec. 10, 1894.

in June, 1895, but until that date pure communism existed only in those goods held by the colony or donated to it; individuals could own private property outside the colony's fences just as they could, to a small extent, within.

A considerable part of Altruria's support stemmed from subordinate councils, a network of local clubs in San Francisco, Oakland, Berkeley, San Jose, Pasadena, and Los Angeles. These clubs had been projected as a part of the initial venture in Berkeley in 1894, and a model constitution for the subsidiary councils had been drafted along with that of the central colony. Several local clubs had been established before the first colonists moved into Sonoma County. By 1895, Pasadena, probably the smallest group, had seventeen members. In theory the colony represented but one unit, although the central and dominant one, in this web of Altrurian clubs, bound together by common ideals, a newspaper, and obligations in the form of dues which the lesser units paid into the central treasury at the colony. The locals also contributed gifts like a cow sent to Altruria as a Christmas present from the San Francisco club or the chess and checker games donated by members in Los Angeles. More important to the parent group, however, the local bodies screened prospective colonists. According to the constitution, any comrade accepted by the central colony should have advanced to it from membership in one of the smaller organizations. The rule was not consistently enforced, but in theory the novitiate could thus prepare himself in the colony's ideals and allow experienced members to decide whether he would make acceptable material. The Keese family from Pasadena, for example, progressed in this way from the smaller unit upward to the colony.

The subordinate councils did not devote their entire time to the affairs of the central colony. In their own right they functioned as study groups, propagating the ideals of Altrurian socialism through lectures and debates. They organized local co-operative ventures, as when the San Francisco Council in December, 1894, established the Altruria Exchange, a full-scale co-operative grocery at 124 Eighth Street. The following June the

Oakland Council founded the Altruria Co-operative Union, a comprehensive scheme including a grocery store, bakery, and laundry with other services projected.[14] This Oakland union eventually absorbed the San Francisco store and did its best to attract trade from Altrurian sympathizers in the farming areas of the Bay hinterland.

Meanwhile financial affairs at the colony itself began to cause alarm. Shortly after the first arrivals, the leaders warned that the colony should admit only those additional members who could pay their own way through the first winter. Clearly the initial capital was not large enough to provide for economic emergencies. In spite of this warning, the Grand Council throughout the first six months welcomed new members who did not have the necessary financial resources. The construction of the hotel continued to burden the economy by absorbing capital and labor which might have been devoted to more immediately productive use. Colonial production itself remained unco-ordinated and was dissipated in a welter of economically unrewarding pursuits. By the summer of 1895 financial chaos seemed imminent.

In the *Altrurian* of June 3, 1895, the central colony cryptically announced to its friends throughout the state that "Altruria, after seven months of experience, has found it expedient to make a thorough readjustment of its plans." Later in the month, June 24, the paper more clearly explained the financial situation which threatened to plunge the colony into ruin. Two choices, it said, lay open: to continue running in the red, a course which most utopias have pursued heedlessly until beyond help, or to liquidate the main colony and reorganize into smaller units. Accepting the latter plan, the original colony officially closed its books, and its members divided into at least three groups. A band of sixteen departed in a remarkably cheerful, courageous, and co-operative manner for an eighty-acre farm west of Cloverdale which James Aitken had purchased for a new colony site.[15] Another section

---

[14]*By-laws of the Altruria Co-operative Union of Oakland, Calif.* (Oakland, 1895); in Bancroft Library, Berkeley.

[15]*Illustrated Atlas of Sonoma County, Calif.* (Santa Rosa, 1897), p. 16.

moved to Santa Rosa and attempted to exist as a co-operative unit within that town. Fourteen members remained at Altruria, continuing to publish the newspaper and acting as a clearing house for the scattered Altrurians.[16]

The financial situation had apparently become so impossible that the prospects of recovery in the existing situation had completely faded. The Altrurians sought by the dispersion to liquidate their debts and thereafter to establish smaller units on a firmer financial footing.[17] Early plans had envisioned a vast plexus of small, co-operating colonies, so the dispersal could be rationalized as progress toward original goals. Some lands must have been sold for purposes of liquidation, since after the reorganization only a few members could be accommodated at the old colony site. Never numbering more than twenty, this revised settlement at Altruria rewrote its by-laws to require slower increases in membership and a more authoritarian system of work allotments. But the earlier enthusiasm had dimmed. All of the segments—at Altruria, Santa Rosa, and near Cloverdale—discontinued communal life within a year. The dispersion of June, 1895, marked in effect the end of the colony experiment.

The Altrurians had parted happily and with little rancor at this inglorious ending of their idealistic plan. They refused to reproach themselves, blaming instead the external competitive economy and the depression years into which their colony had been born. "The difficulties of our financial problem are precisely those of many people and numberless business enterprises, namely the difficulties arising out of the stress of hard times."[18]

Altruria might charge external depression, but it could not blame outside hostility for its downfall. The press was relatively kind, at least in comparison with the animosity that Fountain

---

[16]Articles of Incorporation of this reduced group were filed Dec. 14, 1895, Clerk's Office, Sonoma County Courthouse, Santa Rosa; Document No. 437.

[17]Morrison Swift, "Altruria," *Overland Monthly*, XXIX (June, 1897), 643, stated that another reason for the dispersion was the inability of the acreage to support the larger number of members, but in the same article (p. 644) he referred to weekly loads of excess produce marketed by the colony in Santa Rosa.

[18]*Altrurian*, June 24, 1895.

Grove or Point Loma suffered. Ambrose Bierce aimed a few sarcastic barbs at the members:

Of the amiable asses who have founded the "Altrurian" colony at Mark West it ought to be sufficient to explain that their scheme is based upon the intellectual diversions of such humorists as Plato, More, Fourier, Bellamy and Howells. That assures the ludicrous fizzle of the enterprise.... It will be observed by those who attach meaning to words that this [their official newspaper] is the familiar jargoning of the customary and ever recurrent fool who cometh up as a flower of reform, gorgeous, exuberant and ephemeral."[19]

President David Starr Jordan of Stanford also publicly criticized the community and its ideals,[20] but these isolated statements represented no concerted attack.

By one definition, at least, Altruria succeeded. A few months before the dispersion a visitor remarked, "They are already a success—for they are happy."[21] A short-lived, characteristically vivacious colony, Altruria died with the same transcendent faith with which it had been born.

[19]In his weekly column "Prattle," San Francisco *Examiner*, Oct. 21, 1894.
[20]Berkeley *Herald*, Sept. 25, 1895.
[21]*Altrurian*, April 29, 1895.

CHAPTER 7

Llano del Rio

I N 1895 when the manager of the Altrurian co-operative store in San Francisco resigned in order to move to Altruria itself, a local socialist by the name of Job Harriman succeeded him. Simultaneously, Harriman became president of the Altruria Sub-Council Number Five. Bright and earnest, the thirty-four-year-old socialist had already achieved a leading position in the radical circles of San Francisco. He spoke frequently at labor and socialist gatherings and upheld the socialist position against the single tax in debates with congressmen. Carefully following events at Altruria, he often visited the colony and probably knew as well as Payne himself the financial problems and organizational snags in the functioning of utopia. Nevertheless, like other good Altrurians, he refused to associate the end of the colony with failure of its principles, and, nurturing the ideal for over fifteen years, he eventually led a band of discontented southern Californians into the most extensive and in some ways the most successful secular utopia California has known.

Job Harriman, born in Indiana in 1861, was raised on a farm to the age of eighteen.[1] His schooling reached the college level at Northwestern Christian University (later Butler College) in Indianapolis, where he studied for the ministry. There is no record of his graduation, but after leaving college he found many of his ideas uncongenial to the ministry and he therefore switched into

[1]For details of Harriman's life see J. C. Bates, ed., *History of the Bench and Bar of Calif.* (San Francisco, 1912), p. 343; "Job Harriman," *Who's Who in America, 1918-19;* P. D. Noel, "Job Harriman Finally Is At Rest," *Labor Press* (Los Angeles), Oct. 30, 1925; T. W. Williams, "A Short History of the Socialist Movement in Calif.," Los Angeles *Citizen,* Sept. 1, 1911; "Harriman Funeral Tomorrow," Los Angeles *Times,* Oct. 28, 1925. The *Altrurian,* Feb. 4, 1895, gives a few details of Harriman's connection with that group.

law, attending for a short period Colorado College at Colorado Springs, Colorado. In 1885 he was admitted to practice in the state of Indiana, and the following year, still a foot-loose bachelor, he moved to California.

Although he first registered as a Democrat, the same ideas which earlier alienated him from the ministry probably now weakened his allegiance to the traditional parties, and about 1890 clear indications of his interest in socialism emerged. He joined a Nationalist Club in San Francisco in the early nineties, and with a group of Nationalists in 1892 or 1893 he petitioned and received from the Socialist Labor Party a charter for a local unit. During the nineties he worked his way upward into the higher echelons of the Socialist Labor Party in San Francisco and associated himself for awhile with the Altrurians in their schemes for colonization and consumers' co-operation. In 1898 he stood as the socialist nominee for governor of the state, but he polled only 5,143 votes of 287,064 cast.[2] The socialists of California remained loyal to Harriman, however, and the following year he was made state organizer for the Socialist Labor Party.[3]

Meanwhile in 1899 Harriman had accepted nomination for the presidency of the United States from the Socialist-Laborites. However, as a result of the negotiations for union between the Socialist Labor Party and the Social Democrats, the united socialists, henceforth known as the Socialist Party, drafted a new slate which dropped Harriman to the vice-presidential spot in favor of Eugene V. Debs for president.

During this campaign, Harriman came to believe that the socialist movement needed an economic rather than a purely political base. He began to advocate such requirements for membership in the Socialist Party as previous enrollment in a labor union.

[2]*California Blue Book: or State Roster, 1899* (Sacramento, Calif., [1899]), p. 227.

[3]*Who's Who in America, 1918-19*, stated that Harriman was organizer for the Social Democracy in 1899, but T. W. Williams, Los Angeles *Citizen*, Sept. 1, 1911, referred to the party as the Socialist Labor Party. In the light of Harriman's nominations for the governorship of California in 1898 and for the presidency of the U.S. in 1899, both by the Socialist Labor Party, it seems only likely that the *Who's Who* account was in error.

Subsequently, while practicing criminal law in Los Angeles, he continued to press his new ideas at socialist and labor meetings and among his friends. During the metal workers' strike on the Pacific Coast in 1910, the socialist units of Los Angeles organized to aid labor and Harriman considered such co-operation an excellent economic base for politics. At the same time socialists and labor unions united, as they had for the strike, behind Job Harriman's candidacy for mayor of Los Angeles.

In the early morning hours of October 1, 1910, in Ink Alley behind the building of the Los Angeles *Times*, a bomb exploded killing twenty men and turning the eyes of the nation on southern California. Harrison Gray Otis, editor of the *Times*, had for years been leading conservative forces against organized labor in Los Angeles. In the political campaign of 1910 he had bitterly attacked Harriman and his labor supporters. Understandably enough, the *Times* immediately blamed the union elements of Los Angeles for the crime. Ortie McManigal, James B. and John J. McNamara, labor union organizers from the Midwest who had purportedly been assigned the job in Los Angeles as part of a nation-wide conspiracy, were tracked down and arrested. Labor throughout the country rallied to the defense of its brethren, throwing dimes and dollars into a McNamara Fund for the expected lengthy trial. Clarence Darrow accepted the defense and Job Harriman, already at work on the case, remained as one of Darrow's chief counselors.[4]

The McNamara trial in Los Angeles never progressed beyond jury selection. On the morning of December 1, the McNamara brothers reversed themselves and pleaded guilty. The dramatic somersault, occurring as it did only five days before the municipal polling, placed election beyond hope for Harriman. He received,

[4]Excellent brief accounts of the bombing of the *Times* will be found in Robert Glass Cleland, *California in Our Time* (N.Y., 1947), pp. 67-87; John Walton Caughey, *California* (N.Y., 1940), pp. 569-74; and Ira B. Cross, *A History of the Labor Movement in California* (Berkeley, Calif., 1935), pp. 282-84. See also Louis Adamic, *Dynamite* (2nd ed., N.Y., 1934), pp. 179-253. For complete transcription of the evidence as it was finally tried in Indianapolis, see United States vs. Frank M. Ryan, *et al*, Oct. 3-Dec. 17, 1912; Huntington Library MS. 1152.

Job Harriman

Llano del Rio: A PORTION OF THE SETTLEMENT

Llano del Rio: MAY DAY PARADE

nevertheless, 51,423 votes of 136,915 cast.[5] Harriman would probably have been elected had it not been for the McNamara confes-
sion, but after this upset he never again entered the political arena.

The defeat served to intensify in Harriman's mind the need
for an economic rather than a political base for spreading the
socialist word. Socialism, he thought, needed a concrete example
of successful co-operative life. "It became apparent to me that
a people would never abandon their means of livelihood, good
or bad, capitalistic or otherwise, until other methods were developed which would promise advantages at least as good as those
by which they were living."[6]

Thus thinking, Harriman began to search southern California
for a likely community site. He discovered a nearly defunct company which owned a large tract of land in the Antelope Valley,
an arm of the Mojave Desert nudging into the San Gabriel Mountains. This Mescal Water and Land Company was willing to sell
its stock cheap, and Harriman, interesting five families, including
those of Chester Page and Bert Moore, was able to make a small
down payment on the transaction.[7] He advertised his project in
socialist papers of Los Angeles. As early as May, 1914, members
of the new colony were settling on the land, and in December
"the annual meeting of the stockholders of the Mescal Company
was held in the assembly hall and was the occasion for an enthusiastic rally."[8]

[5]Final returns, Los Angeles *Times,* Dec. 7, 1911.

[6]Harriman in Introduction to Ernest S. Wooster, *Communities of the Past
and Present* (Newllano, Louisiana, 1924), p. iii. Hereafter cited as Wooster, *Communities.*

[7]Wooster, *Communities,* p. 119, refers to the cost as $80,000. Alexander J.
McDonald, a member of the colony, in *The Llano Co-operative Colony and
What It Taught* (Leesville, La., 1950), p. 15, says $80,000 was required to buy
the stock eventually, indicating that it was probably bought in small blocks
as the capital of the group increased. Wooster in *Sunset,* LIII (July, 1924), p. 21,
referred to $150,000 of water district stock, presumably par value, which was
bought at a much smaller price.

[8]*Western Comrade,* II (Dec., 1914), 17. This meeting elected the following
officers: Job Harriman, pres.; F. P. McMahon and A. F. Snell, vice-pres.; W. A.
Engle, secy.; G. P. McCorkle, treas. The Board of Directors was composed
of these five plus David Cederstrom and L. C. Dawson.

Late in 1914, presumably in order to keep pace with a rapidly expanding colony, to proceed under a more accurate statement of purpose, and to increase the amount of capitalization, the Llano del Rio Company was incorporated, the name adapted from the Spanish designation of a nearby creek, and the Mescal stock was transferred to the new corporation. The colony had grown phenomenally fast. Within a few months the handful of initial families had mushroomed to a hundred, and within three years Llano had nearly nine hundred members.[9]

Some of this growth can be attributed to a stock agent, C. V. Eggleston, who was a member of the colony but specially commissioned by the company to sell stock. Needing capital desperately to fulfill its initial obligations, the colony considered such capitalistic promotion a regrettable but essential expedient. Theoretically the purchaser of stock was subject to the approval of the Board of Directors of the company, but financial exigencies often left the theory unobserved. Eggleston, too, was charged to be careful as to the people he approached, but apparently he was not overly cautious; after a few months of his activities, the community discharged him. The growth can be explained more satisfactorily by Harriman's leading position among the laborers and radicals not only of Los Angeles but of the country as a whole. Many supporters too loyal to have been deflected by the McNamara confessions eagerly followed their leader into an economic Eden. Harriman had received thirty-five per cent of the votes cast in 1911, indicating a far from negligible support for him in Los Angeles even after the McNamara trial.

As at Kaweah, the members were largely socialists or labor union members. The publications of the colony usually used the terms colonist and socialist almost synonymously. A. R. Clifton's

[9]U. S. Bureau of Labor Statistics, *Monthly Review*, II (Jan., 1916), 19, stated that the resident members as of that date numbered between 600 and 700. Los Angeles *Times*, Jan. 9, 1916, quoting the Bowman Report (see below, this chap., fn. 19), numbered the colony at 650 in 1916. A. R. Clifton, "History of the Communistic Colony Llano del Rio," Historical Society of Southern California, *Annual Publications*, XI (1918), 82, referred to 900 residents on Aug. 1, 1917.

analysis of the members made at the colony listed the following previous occupations of heads of households:

Farming	100	Clerking	10
Business	73	Mining	8
Factory work	18	Transportation	6
Professions	15	Printing	5
Building	13		

Of this number he estimated that from sixty to seventy per cent had come from west of the Rocky Mountains, and about twenty-five per cent from California.[10]

During the first months of colonial existence, housing presented the most pressing problem. Fortunately, tents and temporary structures furnished adequate shelter, not only at first but during most of the years in California, because of the warm days and balmy nights of a desert climate. A few houses of sun-dried, adobe brick provided protection against summer heat, but these did not rise quickly enough to meet the need.[11] The first community building, the hotel, combined cobblestone foundations with native boulders and frame walls. This structure, in addition to living quarters for bachelors and arriving members, contained a large dining room-assembly hall with fireplaces. Colonists gathered around these hearths on cool winter evenings before blazing juniper fires.

All stockholders theoretically held the same amount of stock, received an equal wage, and lived at and produced for the colony. An entering member must purchase 2,000 shares of stock; he could own no more and no less and, in order to buy any, he must agree to reside at the colony. He could take three-fourths of his shares on credit, $500 cash being the minimum requirement. The remaining $1,500 was payable over a six-year term from the earnings of the colonist.[12]

[10]Historical Society of Southern California, *Annual Publications*, XI (1918), 90. For a similar estimate see McDonald, *Llano Co-operative Colony*, p. 20.

[11]*Llano Colonist* (Llano, Calif.), Apr. 21, 1917.

[12]The minimum requirement was raised in successive jumps till it reached $1,000 about the time of the move to Louisiana in 1917. "Llano Co-operative Colony," U. S. Bureau of Labor Statistics, *Monthly Review*, XXXII (May, 1931), 104.

The colony on its part promised to the entering co-operator continuous employment at wages of four dollars a day. One of the four dollars could apply on the unpurchased stock; the other three were credited to the colonist to be paid in cash when and if the company realized excess profits. The colonist further contracted to charge his food, clothing, and shelter against his credit-account at prices as near cost as feasible.[13]

The wage agreement gradually broke down. As years passed with no excess profits, the credits came to be called "dobey money," after adobe walls which melted away if a trickle of water reached them from the roof. The bookkeeping system became excessively complicated as membership swelled. But the most telling reason for abandoning the wage system in the minds of the colony's leaders was the kind of member it interested. A four-dollar-a-day wage plus guaranteed security was alluring bait,[14] and men attracted by such a materialistic inducement were not always those whose ideals were sufficiently lofty to carry them through the dry years of co-operative hardship. For all of these reasons, an arrangement more like Icaria or Altruria superseded the wage system, the community came to guarantee to each member the necessities of life regardless of his credit account, and the communal aspects thus became progressively more marked.[15]

Most members were in fact less conscious of wages than ideals. The idealistic radical fringe of society provided the colony with its leadership; men like Franklin E. Wolfe, editor of the *Western Comrade*, W. A. Engle, chairman of the Central Labor Council

[13]"Agreement to Purchase Stock and Agreement of Employment," Dec. 1, 1916; uncatalogued Huntington Library MS.

[14]Four dollars a day was about an average wage for skilled labor in 1914. Bricklayers were earning almost $7.00 a day in San Francisco and carpenters almost $5.00. On the other hand, bakers, blacksmiths in railroad shops and street railway employees were making $3.50 a day or less. Teamsters went as low as $2.00, and farm laborers earned something between $2.02 a day (1910) and $2.67 (1917), without board. Figures, for either California as a whole or San Francisco, adapted from the U. S. Bureau of Labor Statistics, *History of Wages in the United States from Colonial Times to 1928* (Washington, D.C., 1929).

[15]E. S. Wooster, "They Shared Equally," *Sunset*, LIII (July, 1924), 22. See also his "Inside a Co-operative Colony," *Nation*, CXVII (Oct. 10, 1923), 378-80.

of Los Angeles, or Frank P. McMahon, former official of the Brick Layers' Union. Many, like Ed Merrill, artist-beekeeper, had lived jail-sprinkled days with the I.W.W. Others, like Chet Page who had been raised in Topolobampo, had joined earlier colonies, one member counting Llano his seventh colony venture. Nearly forty per cent of the members were former farmers who, like Dad Thomas and the Crawford family, had wearied of lonesome toil and had been warmed by Harriman's co-operative promise. The steady farm element which tended to stick to the colony through all the hard years, probably caused Ernest Wooster, long-time Llano leader, to decry the "vehement socialists" and "professional propagandists" who by contrast proved comparatively hopeless as colony material.[16]

Llano achieved remarkable agricultural results. The original land was sandy and porous and dotted with sparse but tenacious desert vegetation. Nevertheless, like California's more southerly Imperial Valley then in its early stages of reclamation, the warm climate would compensate for inadequate soil, and, with water, abundant crops could be produced. Llano had secured water rights to Big Rock Creek (formerly known as Rio del Llano) along with its original purchases of stock from the Mescal Water and Land Company. Co-operative muscle gradually cleared the area of creosote and burro bush and Joshua tree and subsequently ran ditches of creek water to the fields. Rakes pulled hundreds of wagonloads of stones from one small area alone. Alfalfa was the first large-scale planting and eventually spread over four hundred acres. The colony had hoped to produce pears as a staple crop, but its hundred acres of orchards were its most disappointing farming venture. Two hundred acres in corn, the same number in nursery and truck gardens and a few acres of grain made up the balance of nearly two thousand acres cultivated in 1917. As might be expected under the conditions of soil, climate, and water, the yields were not uniformly good, yet the United States Bureau of Labor Statistics in its *Monthly Review* of Janu-

[16]Wooster, *Sunset*, LIII (Sept., 1924), 80.

ary, 1916, reported that the colony during its first year produced seventy-five per cent of the food it consumed and in 1916 was producing about ninety per cent. The total agrarian accomplishment cannot fail to inspire respect, and the prosperous condition of the Antelope Valley to this day may in part be explained by Llano's agricultural pioneering.

Even if the land had produced a marketable excess, the problem of transportation presented a hurdle. Llano lay twenty miles from Palmdale, the nearest railroad connection, and its equipment included only two trucks which could be used for moving produce to the station. Conceivably the output could have been trucked the seventy miles into Los Angeles, but the machines were needed for more immediate agricultural operations on the farm. Llano did export a few small handcraft items, such as rag rugs and knit underwear, but the economy never developed sufficiently to require extensive export relations with the surrounding area.

No single element of Llano life caused such trouble as did the political organization of the colony. Authority stemmed basically from the Articles of Incorporation, first of the Mescal Company and later of the Llano del Rio Company. State law required a board of directors for the corporation and this board of seven (later nine) men, legally responsible to the state, tended toward efficient action. It appointed a superintendent and through him managed the economic and political affairs of the colony.

Unfortunately for efficiency, however, the board was not the ultimate source of political power. The real control lay in the hands of the body of stockholders, the members of the colony, and this group, electing the officers and the Board of Directors, formulating policies, and dictating to the superintendent, came to call itself the General Assembly. The Assembly assumed its powers with a vengeance, never hesitating to dispute decisions of the Board of Directors. It met fortnightly in the dining hall and the sessions often lasted from after supper to midnight or even till two o'clock in the morning. Pet projects, personal quarrels, and jealousies were all aired. Dozens of resolutions passed each session, many to be discarded two weeks later. Sensing the incompleteness of articles of incorporation as political instruments, the Assembly attempted to draft for itself a constitution, drawing up a forty-page document. Every conceivable contingency was covered in it, but the legislative body discussed and quibbled over its details for such an interminable time that the whole project foundered.[17] In the words of Ernest Wooster, one of its members, the General Assembly was "Democracy rampant, belligerent, unrestricted,"

an inquisition, a mental pillory, a madhouse of meddlesomeness..., a jumble of passions and idealism—and all in deadly earnest.... It became a [monster] which threatened to destroy the colony.... The General Assembly was democracy with the lid off.[18]

The political organ which functioned most effectively and consequently assumed larger and larger powers was the Board of Managers, the foremen of the departments, appointed by the superintendent. They met informally every evening to report the progress of the day, to plan the next day's work, to exchange necessary men and teams and tools. The concreteness and urgency of the work apparently inspired its members to quiet efficiency. Later in the colony's life the Board of Managers tended to merge into the Board of Directors with considerably more power granted to a general manager, in place of the earlier superintendent.

During 1915 a discontented element named itself the Welfare League and sought to launch a new political system. They charged that Job Harriman as president dominated the Board of Directors and was imposing a more and more dictatorial regime. The Welfare League wished to supplant Harriman and the board with a complete democracy in which every decision, legislative or execu-

[17]Llano never had a constitution, technically so called. It did have a simple declaration of principles and a pledge which together added to little more than a preamble. For the declaration, see Wooster, *Communities,* pp. 132-33. For the pledge, see Robert C. Brown, *Can We Co-operate?* (Pleasant Plains, N.Y., 1940), pp. 99-102.

[18]*Sunset,* LIII (July, 1924), 81.

tive, would be made by the combined membership in General Assembly. The Board of Directors rejected the idea, and the Welfare League, planning its approach to win the General Assembly, met in caucus outdoors behind the creosote bushes. As they entered the assembly wearing sprigs of brush in lapels and hats, they came to be called "the brush gang" or "brushers." Though their plan failed, their name was ever thereafter applied to disgruntled groups of members.

The brush gang was not silenced, however, and it petitioned the State Commissioner of Corporations for an investigation. As a consequence, H. M. Bowman, deputy commissioner of Los Angeles, presented on December 31, 1915, a harsh and critical report, but no grounds were found for revocation of the Llano charter.[19] Thereupon, thirty-two colonists withdrew, declaring the colony a one-man autocracy dominated by Harriman.

Llano, however, was not deeply affected by the demissions. By 1917 over sixty departments functioned under division managers. A representative list of economic activities included: agriculture, architecture and surveying, art studio, bakery, barber shop, bee-keeping, cabinet shop, cannery, cleaning and pressing, clearing, fencing, and grading land, dairy, fish hatchery, general store, hay and grain, hogs, horses and teaming, the hotel, irrigation, laundry, lime kiln, library, machine shop, medical department, poultry, printing, post office, rabbits, rugs, sawmill, sanitation, shoe shop, soap factory, tannery, tractors, transportation, tin shop, wood and fuel.[20]

An individual member reported for work in the department to which the Board of Managers assigned him. The managers frequently switched men from job to job, thus opening themselves to charges of favoritism and discrimination. They main-

[19]The Division of Corporations, State of California, Los Angeles, while clearing old files, destroyed on July 17, 1930, the papers of the Llano Company, numbered in their records LA-747. The original Bowman Report was lost along with these papers. For newspaper accounts of the report see Los Angeles *Times*, Jan. 9, 1916, and a good discussion in the San Francisco *Examiner* for the same date.

[20]*Western Comrade*, V (May, 1917), 9.

tained, however, that in addition to meeting seasonal and other irregular demands, frequent transfers tended to eliminate stigmas attaching to particular jobs. Slackers appeared occasionally in each department, Comrade Gibbons providing a notorious example. A former member of the I. W. W. and a constant spouter of propaganda, Gibbons was afflicted with mysterious aches and pains, none of which ever showed external evidence, but all of which kept him from active work. His complaint came to be called "gibbonitis," which for years designated a shirker in the colony's vernacular.

The Llano co-operative store, supplying as it did almost all the members' food and clothing, suffered constant criticism. In the agreement with each new member, the colony promised to furnish supplies as near cost as possible, carefully stipulating, however, that unusual transportation and overhead expenses must be taken into account. The Bowman Report pointed to hats selling for two dollars which cost the colony twenty-five cents and meals worth nine cents being priced at twenty-five. It is hard to know whether such accusations were true, and, if true, whether any justification existed for higher prices in these instances. No similar indictments were made after the Bowman Report and the withdrawal of the thirty-two dissidents, and, in any case, the co-operative store gradually metamorphosed into little more than a dispensary as the more communal system gradually replaced wages and credits.

One hundred and twenty-five children in 1917 attended the Llano schools. The colony had cause to be proud of its educational system, based as it was on a high set of ideals.

... the training of children must be conducted in such manner as to induce the unfoldment of the ethical and spiritual nature. Failure so to do means the destruction of the Community itself. . . . The child's mind must be free from the influence of dogmas and kept in a receptive and scientific attitude. . . .[21]

---

[21]Harriman in Introduction to Wooster, *Communities*, p. vii.

The system had three distinct elements: the public, Montessori, and Industrial Schools. A child reaching school age entered first the Montessori School. Around 1900 Madame Maria Montessori had organized infant schools in a series of model tenements in Rome. Her methods, leaning heavily on sense training and individual freedom, spread rapidly over Europe and into the United States and were heralded as a striking improvement over traditional approaches. The Llano kindergarten was one of the first and largest Montessori schools in California.[22]

For the elementary grades the system submitted to the regular county and state curricula, received tax funds, and accepted the regulations of the county superintendent. But the colony added another dimension to education in the form of an Industrial School. A pet project of George Pickett, later superintendent of the colony, this school came also to be known as the Junior Colony or the Kid Kolony. Here the high-school-age students learned a trade, produced as they learned, and in general approached theory only through practice. The boys studied the handling and care of tools and livestock while the girls learned cooking and sewing.[23]

Adults attended night-school classes or read from a library of several thousand volumes. If less intellectually inclined, they joined the gun club or the mandolin club or performed with the orchestra or the brass band. Baseball teams played intra-colonial games. Dances occupied two evenings a week, Thursdays for the children, Saturdays for the adults. If more sedentary in his habits, a colonist could sit before the fire in the hotel and listen to the discussion and unfolding of innumerable projects and curious schemes: a venture to mine for gold in nearby Black Butte or

[22]For a picture of the school with its teacher and children, see *Llano Viewbook* (Llano, 1917), p. [22]. Prudence S. Brown, Llano educational leader, "Liberty and Play for Baby," *Western Comrade*, V (May, 1917), 19; "Montessorians," *ibid.*, III (Feb., 1916), 22; "Montessori—What It Achieves," *ibid.*, V (Aug., 1917), 13.

[23]Mildred G. Buxton, another of the educational leaders at Llano, "Children and Livestock," *Western Comrade*, IV (Dec., 1916), 22; "Education for Real Life," *ibid.*, IV (Nov., 1916), 21.

a proposal to plant acres of turnips as a certain and profitable staple. Here he could talk with the pioneer aviator whose home-built plane was taking shape in the meadow or the water witch with the unerring willow wand.

Social life was full, as can be judged from a May Day celebra-tion and a typical Sunday-evening program. The May Day festivities of 1917 commenced at nine o'clock in the morning with intra-community athletic events, including a Fat Women's Race. The entire group of colonists then formed a Grand Parade and marched to the hotel where the Literary Program followed. The band played from a bunting-draped grandstand, the choral society sang appropriate revolutionary anthems like the "Marseillaise," and founder Harriman addressed the assembled multitude. All then moved into the Almond Grove for a barbecue dinner. After supper, a group of young girls injected the English into the radical tradition by dancing about the May Pole. At 7:30 the dramatic club presented "Mishaps of Minerva" with newly decorated scenery in the assembly hall. Dancing consumed the remainder of the evening. Late that same month the regular Sunday-evening program included the following attractions:

The Llano Orchestra in Several Selections

* * *

The Mixed Quartet

* * *

The Mandolin Trio

* * *

Speech on Life at Equality Colony by a Former Member

* * *

Junior Dramatic Club in
"Lovebird's Matrimonial Agency"

* * *

The Choral Society Accompanied by the Entire Orchestra
in the Anvil Chorus from *Il Trovatore*.

It was well that the social life sparkled, for work was hard and the food at table often scanty. Weeks went by with no other vegetable than carrots. Yet enthusiasm did not die; indeed it seemed to be contagious, for in one year over two thousand outsiders visited the colony.[24] Nevertheless, one problem could not be solved by enthusiasm, the problem of water, which rose to haunt the expanding population.

Nothing could be more crucial to the development of a desert area than water. Harriman knew this and wisely secured water-rights to Big Rock Creek along with the stock of the Mescal Water and Land Company. Engineers estimated that at least 20,000 acres of land could be irrigated from the available water.[25] This enormous supply of water could be tapped in dependable fashion only by the building of a dam, by the sinking of strategic wells, and by tunneling and piping to avoid seepage. The colonists constructed wells and ditches lined with cement and cobblestones, but the dam was never built.

In the course of the years a series of disappointing facts came to light. A dam, it was discovered, would provide a reservoir of considerably smaller content than had been originally expected. Furthermore, the underground flow beneath the foothill washes was disappointingly small, a situation caused, it was later learned, by an earthquake fault which diverted much of the water in an unexpected direction. Coupled with these disappointments came a series of lawsuits in which neighboring ranchers disputed Llano's riparian rights.

The seriousness of the water problem set Harriman and other leaders casting about for the possibilities of a new location. While dickering over a spot in the San Joaquin Valley, the colonists entertained a visiting socialist lecturer, Jake Rhodes, who told them of a bargain near Leesville in west-central Louisiana. The Gulf Lumber Company offered 20,000 acres of partially timbered land, including the site of an old mill town known as Stables,

---

[24]Wooster, "Bread and Hyacinths," *Sunset*, LIII (Aug., 1924), 21.

[25]U. S. Bureau of Labor Statistics, *Monthly Review*, II (Jan., 1916), 20. *Llano Colonist* (Newllano, La.), Feb. 18, 1933.

for $120,000. The buildings of the town would provide initial shelter and a base from which to expand. In October of 1917 Job Harriman headed a committee which journeyed to Louisiana to view the prospects and arrange for an extended period of payments. The deal was concluded, and Llano had a second home which it christened Newllano.

Plans called for the retention of the colony in California as the profitable base for the support of a smaller number of members. By 1918, however, its economy was so badly shaken by the move and its trustee, G. P. McCorkle, had mismanaged its affairs so seriously that involuntary bankruptcy proceedings were instituted in the United States District Court of Los Angeles. Harriman, hastening back from Louisiana, was able to effect a reduction in the deficiency judgment, but the court decision closed the colony in California and weighted the Louisiana venture with heavy indebtedness.[26]

At least a hundred of the California members followed the colony to Louisiana, boarding automobiles or a specially chartered train for the continental trek.[27] Another troop of twenty-five families converged on Newllano from Texas, a party assembled by James D. Scoggins, a real estate agent who had maneuvered the transaction and from whom Rhodes had first heard of the land. Many of the Texans were illiterate and, if they understood a co-operative colony at all, glimpsed only the rosy aspects of it. The first year of life in Louisiana witnessed recurrent conflicts between the Californians and the Texans. When the latter withdrew, they dragged Llano into court again, but an agreement

[26]McDonald, *Llano Co-operative Colony*, p. 73, agrees with Wooster (*Communities*, p. 127) that the debt carried over from California was between $12,000 and $17,000. See also U. S. Bureau of Labor Statistics, *Monthly Review*, XXXII (May, 1931), 101-102. For the trial see Los Angeles *Times* and San Francisco *Chronicle*, Aug. 2, 1918; and for Harriman's statements about it, see Wooster, *Communities*, pp. 126-27.

[27]Walter Millsap maintains that over 600 of the California colonists eventually ended up in Newllano, La.; he says that the train itself included over six packed cars and that an uncounted number of additional members hitch-hiked or traveled the best way they could. Letter to the author, Feb. 5, 1952. McDonald, *Llano Co-operative Colony*, p. 23, refers to 65 adults who made the move.

between the disputants left the colony free, though more in debt.

In retrospect, the deep South was a regrettable choice for a locale. The colonists, largely westerners with radical economic ideas, tended to express equally radical social views. They proclaimed equality and would refuse nothing to the Negro which they would not also refuse to the white. When one of the colonists applied at the local courthouse for a marriage license, he filled in the "color" blank with the word "Red."[28] Louisiana society, intent as it was on the distinction between black and white, would not have appreciated the joke, and yet Newllano depended economically on this society. Since co-operative colonies have usually received most of their support and recruitment from their local areas, such ideological conflict must have hampered Newllano to a sizable extent.

In the decade following 1919 Newllano slowly consolidated its gains. Membership varied, rising abruptly in 1920, decreasing thereafter, but increasing again in the early thirties to about four hundred. Three outside auxiliary units supplied the central colony with rice, citrus fruit, and cattle.[29]

Nevertheless, financial solvency was slow of attainment, and the depression descended before the colony's strength was sufficient to withstand it. In the early thirties unemployed flocked to the colony. Entrance fees were suspended in case after case as Llano came to resemble "a glorified breadline of idealists and opportunists weathering the depression together."[30] In 1935, following a long and destructive "rebellion" led by Eugene D. Carl against the administration of George Pickett, disgruntled members and creditors petitioned the courts to place the colony in receivership. A dirty and disagreeable period followed in which three successive receivers served the court. One of them at least, judging from the following sale figures, perpetrated sizable frauds

[28]Brown, *Can We Co-operate?*, p. 173.

[29]The rice ranch was about 80 miles south of the colony; the others were in Fremont, Texas, and Gila, N.M. For extended descriptions of these by a member, see McDonald, *Llano Co-operative Colony*, pp. 39-43.

[30]Brown, *Can We Co-operate?*, p. 35.

on the colony. The Newllano townsite, sixty-odd acres including homes, the Colony Hotel, hospital, store, theater, printing establishment, machine shop, blacksmith shop, shoe shop, potato dry kiln, filling station, tourist camp, and school buildings—approximately seventy-five buildings with all of their contents, a current value of at least $50,000—was sold for $6,650![31] As late as 1947 the colonists were still enmeshed in the courts, attempting to right the injustice of the final receivership.

George T. Pickett became manager of Newllano in 1920 and remained so to the last. Pickett's assumption of office marked the end of Job Harriman's active direction of Llano affairs. Like his precursor and mentor in co-operation, Edward Payne, Harriman long suffered from tuberculosis, and the dampness of Louisiana coupled with the years of strain severely taxed his health. He returned to California and Sierra Madre, a suburb of Los Angeles where dry air purportedly helped combat lung disease. In seclusion he lived until his death on October 26, 1925, at the age of sixty-four. Knowing Llano still persevered, he died firm of faith in the future fortunes of his intellectual child.

[31]John B. Pollard, *Report on the Llano del Rio Company of Nevada by John B. Pollard, State Farm Debtor Supervisor for the State of Louisiana* (n.p., 1939), p. 2.

CHAPTER 8

Colonies in Short
and After a Fashion

Τ HE remaining utopian colonies of California may be considered subordinate to those already described. Although important for a complete picture, they do not warrant detailed and systematic examination. Some of these communities involved few people or lasted for an unusually short period of time; some left so meager a record that their story remains tantalizingly obscure; some had a significance which lay elsewhere than in the utopian category.

The colony which best fits the latter criterion was also the first religious utopia to appear in California following statehood.

The Latter Day Saints, wrote Joseph Smith, "shall be assembled together unto the place which I have appointed,"[1] and in the early 1850's when the valley of the Great Salt Lake became the Mormon Zion, the Saints throughout the world began to hear the call: "Come home; come to the land of Joseph, to the Valleys of Ephraim." This particular summons was in the General Epistle of 1852, which went on to announce a new route to Salt Lake. "Those who are accustomed to a warm climate, and have the opportunity, may journey to California, and take counsel of the Presidency at San Bernardino; and such will find themselves near home, if they land at San Diego."[2] San Bernardino was the first

[1] *The Book of Doctrine and Covenants* (Liverpool, Eng. [1845]), p. 219.

[2] Eighth General Epistle, Oct. 13, 1852, in *Deseret News* (Great Salt Lake City, Utah Terr.), Oct. 16, 1852; also, w... 1 slight variations, in *Latter-day Saints' Millennial Star* (Liverpool), XV (Feb. 19, 1853), 116.

Thomas Lake Harris at Fountain Grove

Holy City

of a line of proposed settlements reaching from southern California into the heart of the Salt Lake Valley, an artery meant not so much to extend Zion as to help the Saints reach home.

Early in 1851 elders Amasa Lyman and Charles C. Rich had received instructions for "establishing a settlement in the southern part of California, at no great distance from San Diego, and near Williams' ranche and the Cahone Pass."[3] The two elders ranked among the twelve apostles of the church, and the calls they in turn issued to individual followers approximated commands. Ready acceptance of a summons to missionary service played an essential part in Mormon discipline, but Henry Boyle, one of those mustered for San Bernardino, entered in his diary: "Brothers A. Lyman and C. C. Rich have sent for me to get ready and take a mission with them to California. . . . I can truly say I never started anywhere so reluctantly as I start on this journey."[4] Rich himself, though he claimed to go willingly, wrote of the trip, "Never at any time did I leave home under more trying feelings."[5]

Early in June, 1851, after an arduous desert journey, a caravan of nearly 150 wagons and 500 people camped in a sycamore grove at the foot of Cajon Pass. On the twenty-second of September Lyman and Rich negotiated for part of the Rancho San Bernardino, about 35,000 acres, from the Lugo family for $77,500. Only $7,000 was paid on September 22, the two apostles forming themselves into a corporation to assume the remaining debt.

Soon after moving on the new lands, the colonists were faced with Indian hostility which required the construction of a stockade. Completed in December, 1851, the fort housed over a hundred families, mostly in separate dwellings, throughout 1852. During this period the colony resembled a co-operative or socialistic utopia more than at any other time. Communal labor raised the barricades of heavy willow trunks and sycamore, and

[3]*Millennial Star*, XIII (April, 1851), 213.

[4]Henry G. Boyle, "Diary and Journal" (unpub. MS in possession of Mr. N. I. Butt; photostat, 13 vols., in Huntington Library), I, 39 (entries of Feb. 19 and Mar. 1, 1851).

[5]Rich, "Diary," entry of Mar. 12, 1851; unpub. MS in Library of the Church Historian, Salt Lake City.

co-operation built public facilities within and without the fort—irrigation systems, dams, a grist mill, the Bowery for church and school. In the same way the men hewed a sixteen-mile lumber road into the San Bernardino mountains, a feat comparable to the Kaweah road into the Sierras forty years later. In traditional frontier fashion, the men gathered to reap a brother's field or rear his adobe house, assembling at the call of the six-foot horn of Uncle Grief.[6]

The whole community assumed the obligation for paying the debt on the ranch, although the ownership rested in the private corporation, Lyman, Rich, and Company. The mortgage installments were raised in various ways. The company sold lots to individual colonists and received donations of money, grain, or produce; the elders sent prospectors to the Kern River gold fields and missionaries to all parts of the state "to preach the gospel and gather up all the means that could be obtained for to make payment on the Ranch."[7] By such means the Mormons maintained a high credit reputation.

From the beginning the community was a confusing mixture of private business venture and co-operative colony. Many of the communal aspects reflected early necessity—raising the stockade, laying out water systems, and cutting timber for needed construction. As the colonists moved from the fort to individual farms, communal life became less pronounced and private enterprise more evident. For one thing, each plot had to be bought from the central firm of Lyman, Rich, and Company. Other corporations, like Lyman, Rich, Hopkins, and Company, inaugurated business enterprises—lumbering, milling grain, or retailing merchandise. And individualistic endeavor always netted good returns on Mormon butter, eggs, poultry, and cattle, which moved well in Los Angeles markets.[8]

[6]George W. Beattie and Helen P. Beattie, *Heritage of the Valley: San Bernardino's First Century* (Pasadena, Calif., 1939), pp. 186-87, 186 fn.

[7]Boyle, "Diary," I, [41] (entry of July 4, 1855).

[8]Harris Newmark, *Sixty Years in Southern California* (3rd ed., Boston, 1930), p. 88.

The church continued to exert powerful controls, but these fell increasingly into the moral and religious spheres. Like the Puritans of seventeenth-century New England, the Mormons had maintained political hegemony by concentrating ecclesiastical and civil government in the hands of the same men. Rich, president of the church, became also the first mayor of the town. But by 1854, when the city of San Bernardino was incorporated, the elders heard rumblings of discontent. As in New England, the growth of population, especially of Gentiles, and the presence of disgruntled Mormons foreshadowed the weakening of theocracy. When Henry Boyle returned to San Bernardino after a half-year mission to the north, he noted with horror that the colony had become "a den of Apostates, thieves, gamblers, drunkards, Methodists and evry kind of foul Character."[9]

Dissatisfaction burst publicly in 1855 during the spring elections for county supervisors. The governing body of the church, as was customary, had chosen a slate, and all loyal Mormons were expected to second its choice. But Benjamin Grouard and Frederick Van Leuven placed their own names in opposition to the church's candidates. The fury of the hierarchy broke over the heads of the two men. They were called to appear before the assembled church, and Henry Boyle entered in his diary a most revealing description of that meeting.

Brother Lyman proceeded to explain the nature of the wrongs committed by them [Grouard and Van Leuven], and of the evil consequences that would grow out of such a course of conduct. . . . They [the renegades] raised the hue and cry that we were Slaves and not men (because we chose to be united in a principle of riteous conduct.) that had not the privilege of thinking for our selves but was led by one man, without useing our capacity to think independantly of ourselves. For my own part I have always acted upon my own convictions of wright and wrong, and I am convinced that evry good man does in this place. I have too always acted in unison with the Authority and council of this church. The men above mentioned would not confess or retract. Therefore they were cut off from the Church. It is a painfull thing, . . . to see men stuburn and unwilling

9Boyle, "Diary," IV (no page; entry of Dec. 4, 1857); spelling as given.

to do right, ... to see them deliberately lay down the principles of life and salvation, evry thing that is worth living for on this earth, and without which there is no life nor joy, nor assurance nor contentment, nothing that is noble, pure, and Holy, but all, all is a blank, dark and gloomy, too dark for me to think of; it makes the Blood chill in my veins.[10]

Though the backsliders were disfellowshipped, disunity spread and the anti-church party disturbed all subsequent elections. In 1857, concerned with the growing apostasy in San Bernardino and faced with increasing hostility from the United States government and suspicions arising from the Mountain Meadows Massacre, Brigham Young recalled all Mormons to their natural stronghold in the Salt Lake Valley. Hastening to obey, the settlers at San Bernardino sold property at ruinous prices. For Lyman, Rich, and Company the unsold acres of the ranch brought little more than the unpaid mortgage. Many Mormons refused to accept such losses, renounced their faith, and remained. But the great majority loaded their possessions on wagons and moved homeward again to Zion.

For many reasons San Bernardino under the Mormons was not strictly a utopian colony. The mode of life was too much the child of necessity; co-operative living was more an expedient than a social ideal to be continued and expanded. As in the previously mentioned settlement of Anaheim, the communal phases lasted only until conditions permitted the expansion of private enterprise.

On the other hand, Mormon settlements wherever they occurred were utopian in the same way as were the New England Puritan colonies. Like the Puritans, the Mormons believed that the city of God could be created on earth. The Saints had withdrawn successively from New York and Ohio and Illinois far into the western wilderness in order to establish a new religious pattern, and from Salt Lake a small group had withdrawn further to San Bernardino. Yet there was little volition on the part of those sent to California in 1851. The founders of the new settle-

[10]II (no page; entry of April 29, 1855); spelling and grammar as given.

ment came because they had been appointed, and they returned to Utah, not because their venture failed, but simply because they were ordered home. The significance of their experiment lay less in the field of utopianism than in the history of the expansion and contraction of Mormonism in the West.

As the returning Saints settled themselves again in the Salt Lake Valley, half-way around the world in Cracow, Poland, Count Charles Bozenta Chlapowski and his actress-wife, Helena Modjeska,[11] were frequently entertaining a circle of intellectual radicals bitter over Russian domination of their homeland. From this coterie one winter evening in 1875, after a period of excessively oppressive censorship and a siege of ill health for Madame Modjeska, a scheme of emigrating to America was hatched, and in the elated conversations that followed, the plan narrowed to the establishment in California of a utopian colony on the model of the earlier Brook Farm in Massachusetts. Serious meetings through the winter carried the enterprise nearer maturity. The members drafted statutes, vowed to obey their own laws, and pooled financial resources. Madame Modjeska reflected the group's enthusiasm when she described her dreams of California:

'Oh, but to cook under the sapphire-blue sky in the land of freedom! What Joy!' I thought. 'To bleach linen at the brook like the maidens of Homer's "Iliad"! After the day of toil, to play the guitar and sing by moonlight, to recite poems, or to listen to the mocking-bird! And listening to our songs would be charming Indian maidens, our neighbors, making wreaths of luxuriant wild flowers for us! And in exchange we should give them trinkets for their handsome brown necks and wrists! And oh, we should be so far away from every-day gossip and malice, nearer to God, and better.'[12]

The group which eventually left Poland for California consisted of Count Chlapowski, Madame Modjeska, and Rudolphe (later Ralph) Modjeska, son of her first marriage; Henryk Sien-

---

[11]Née Helena Opid; for stage purposes she maintained the name of her first husband, Gustave S. Modjeski, who had died prior to her second marriage.

[12]Helena Modjeska, *Memories and Impressions* (N.Y., 1910), pp. 250-51. Hereafter cited as Modjeska, *Memories*. The basic source.

kiewicz, whose fame as an author rests on his later work, *Quo Vadis?*; Julian Sypniewski, his wife and two children; Paprocki, a painter; and Anusia, a flighty girl of sixteen who had been hired to care for the children.[13] In the early spring of 1876 the group sent two of its members, Sienkiewicz and Sypniewski, to explore the land of southern California. After investigation, the committee chose the area of Anaheim because many citizens of that town spoke German, a familiar language for the Poles. Sypniewski returned to Poland with glowing accounts; Sienkiewicz waited in California at Anaheim Landing writing letters which were no less enticing. In July, 1876, the little band sailed aboard the *Donau* from Bremen. They landed in New York, stopping long enough for an excursion to Washington where they eagerly received boxes of pamphlets on farming from the Department of Agriculture; proceeded to the Isthmus on a steamer which suffered an explosion from a bursting boiler; journeyed from Panama to San Francisco on an antique side-wheeler; and finally entrained for Los Angeles. Reuniting with Sienkiewicz, they made the last lap of their journey in wagons to the ranch near Anaheim.

After the long trek and the glowing prospects, the immigrants arrived at their utopia to find a wooden house of two bedrooms, a dining room, and a parlor with an upright piano and a sofa. To Modjeska "the commonplaceness of it all was painfully discouraging."[14] Sypniewski and his family took the large bedroom; Chlapowski and his wife, the small one; Ralph slept on the parlor sofa; Anusia, in a nook of the kitchen; and Sienkiewicz and Paprocki made shift in the barn.

Utopia suffered problems from the very first morning. Madame Modjeska, who in the assignment of tasks had drawn the

[13]These 9 people are all Madame Modjeska ever mentions as taking part in the colony. Hinds, *American Communities* (3rd ed., Chicago, 1908), p. 445, numbers the colony at 33, a figure which he quoted from an unnamed Los Angeles newspaper. The newspaper, or he himself, may have found the figure in Henry G. Tinsley's article in the San Francisco *Chronicle*, Feb. 27, 1898, which also lists 33 members. It is thoroughly possible that Madame Modjeska in her *Memories*, written 30 years after the event, did not remember all the Poles who joined the colony, but it is doubtful that the number ever went as high as 33.

[14]Modjeska, *Memories*, p. 287.

kitchen, soon learned that even breakfast for a group of intellectual Poles was no simple affair. Each one wanted something
different. Tea, coffee, milk, chocolate, and wine-soup had to be
served every morning, to mention the drink alone.

The first day's work in the fields was glorious—Nature's sons
and daughters returning to her bosom. But on the following
morning lame backs and sore arms kept Nature's children abed.
In the weeks that followed, when muscles reacted better but the
spirit lagged from toil and homesickness, the whole colony often
took to its buggies for a picnic or a drive to Anaheim Landing. It
required the combined efforts of three men to kill a turkey on the
occasion of a festive dinner. Even Sypniewski, the sole possessor
of agricultural experience, had gained his knowledge in a funda-
mentally different soil and climate.

Trouble came and agricultural reverses, but the colony never
lost its high spirits. A visitor reported that he found the men practicing Wagner while a mule and a cow died from improper food.
Another neighbor, Lyman Busby, once said, "You ought to have
seen how jolly they used to be when everything on the farm was
drying up in the sun and the animals were all sick and dying."[15]
Sienkiewicz came gradually to divorce himself from the agricultural labor, setting up a table under the trees in a far corner of
the ranch where he read, smoked, and wrote most of the day.

After six months on the new Brook Farm, the colony counted
$15,000 spent and almost nothing returned. "We all came to the
conclusion," wrote Modjeska, "that our farming was not a success."

We had several cows, but there was no one to milk them, and we
had to buy milk, butter, and cream from the neighbors. We had
chickens, but our fine dogs made regular meals of the eggs. We had
a vineyard, which yielded beautiful muscat grapes, but there was
nobody to buy them, and often people would come and fill their
wagons with them without more ado; they said that such was the
custom of the country. . . . Our winter crop of barley was fast disappearing in the mouths of the neighboring cattle, although I tried
myself to shoot at the latter with my revolver.[16]

[15]San Francisco *Chronicle*, Feb. 27, 1898.
[16]Modjeska, *Memories*, p. 304.

In the spring of 1877 the actress laid down her gun and her skillet, perfected her English, and returned to the stage, paving the way for those triumphs with Edwin Booth and Otis Skinner which placed her so prominently in the history of the American theater. Money from the sale of the farm provided return passage for the other homesick colonists. Madame Modjeska and her family, however, remained in America, building a summer house surrounded by her Forest of Arden in Santiago Canyon, only a few miles from the site where the rudeness of agricultural reality had disrupted a captivating utopian dream.

In the early 1880's Isaac B. Rumford on his farm in Kern County saw in his sleep a heaven-like land where Christianity ruled and men truly loved their neighbors as themselves. He and his wife, Sara, were active reformers for temperance and women's rights, and now, inspired by a dream, they sought a return to fundamental Christianity based on a simpler community life. Prerequisite to this simplicity lay a revolution in eating habits called by the Rumfords the "Edenic Diet." Meat was forbidden along with any provisions touched by fire. "Cooking destroys the vitality of the food, besides being a waste of labor and of time; it makes a slave of the one who cooks and shortens life."[17] On October 14, 1881, Isaac Rumford and his family embarked upon the Edenic Diet. From that day forth they maintained perfect health. Isaac Rumford's chest expanded by two inches, without training, and to all the Rumfords sleep came naturally and easily.

A typical Edenic dinner began with half a pound of "grainia" (oat groats and wheat, ground fine), eaten either dry or moistened with water or fruit juice, and continued with grated apple, mashed almonds, and pounded raisins. Dessert might be flour and water, flavored with vanilla and strawberries, frozen as ice cream. The Rumfords took plenty of time, an hour or more, to enjoy such a dinner, indulged in a social period following the meal, and retired at eleven in the evening to a sound sleep.

[17] *Joyful News Co-operator*, June, 1884. This publication is the main existing source for the Joyful story. Complete file in California State Library, Sacramento.

In January, 1884, Isaac and Sara Rumford printed the first issue of their newspaper, the *Joyful News Co-operator*. The "Joyful" derived from the name of their fruit farm near Bakersfield and the "Co-operator" denoted the nature of the colony which they planned. It would be a utopia based on simple living, rudimentary Christianity, and, above all, "feeding our bodies upon pure, *live* food, that has not been deprived of its magnetic, or best life-giving forces, by fire."[18] The Constitution of the Association of Brotherly Co-operators called for "seeking Truth, and striving to grow into a harmonious condition." Members were to hold shares in the association and an officer must own stock worth at least $182.50. All labor received, somewhat more generously than at Kaweah a few years later, a uniform wage of fifty cents per day. Members should "neither gamble, use profane or vulgar language, use, buy, sell, or give away tobacco, whisky, or other intoxicants except for chemical or agricultural purposes, or do anything that will be a public nuisance."

Prospective colonists met in San Francisco on Saturday afternoons during the early months of 1884. Often the gatherings were combined Edenic Diet and Dress Reform meetings at which times Madame Brownjohn's prize-winning trouser-dress was enthusiastically exhibited.[19] Meanwhile the actual colony itself near Bakersfield materialized on only a small scale. The complexion of one of its early male residents improved so markedly that the girls of Bakersfield called the hapless member "Peaches and Cream." But even as late as November of 1884 only six colonists resided at the farm. "There are six of us here, living on the one meal [per day] Edenic system, with the exception that two or three, will use sometimes a few grapes, a plum, or peach in the morning, and one uses . . . water melon during the day, but the strictest livers get the best results, and our melon eater is the least capable of all, though with more grain, and less melon, he should be, the most so."[20]

[18]This and the following two quotations are from *Joyful News Co-operator*, Feb., 1884; italics *sic*.

[19]*Woman's Herald of Industry* (San Francisco, monthly), Feb., 1884.

[20]*Joyful News Co-operator*, Nov., 1884.

The Rumfords became involved in other reform movements in San Francisco, but they published the *Joyful News Co-operator* throughout the year 1884. The fervor with which editors and contributors debated its questions never waned: Shall salt be a part of the Edenic Diet? Will one meal a day suffice for the true worker in Christ's Kingdom? Meanwhile, with little active support remaining, the Association of Brotherly Co-operators disbanded as a colony late in 1884. Although the Rumfords retained the Edenic Diet as part of a purely commercial and individualistic venture, which they called the Edenic Health Retreat Company, they never again attempted to found utopia on diet reform.[21]

Twice each month during the new and the full moons, the tides which surge through the Golden Gate push up Suisun Bay and the Sacramento River and overflow the low-lying islands in the delta. The land of these islands is moderately useful for pasture but much more valuable if protected by levees and tilled. So reckoned a group of men laboring in 1893 on the dikes surrounding Winters Island near the confluence of the San Joaquin and Sacramento Rivers.

Erastus Kelsey, a leader of the Oakland Nationalist Club during the early 1890's and owner of Winters Island, desired to found and partially endow a co-operative colony along the pattern of Kaweah. He reputedly asked Burnette G. Haskell to organize a community for him, but whether the founder of Kaweah refused or tried and failed is not known. At any rate, Kelsey discovered his desired functionary in Mrs. Kate Lockwood Nevins, an organizer for the Farmer's Alliance in California. She had been born in Ohio in 1855, had studied at the University of Michigan, and had later trained herself as an architect. After arriving in Cali-

---

[21]A precursor to Joyful, similar in its dietetic and religious views, was the Societas Fraternia near Anaheim in 1879. Its leader, a Dr. Schlesinger, was hailed into court in May, 1879, because the neighbors of the colony had charged that a new-born child was slowly starving on a diet of scraped apple, rice, and barley water. The colony lived in a building of circular rooms, which were intended to promote the circulation of air. See *Alta California* (San Francisco), May 27 and 31, 1879.

fornia, she joined the Farmer's Alliance and the Populist Party and so had numerous contacts among reform groups when Erastus Kelsey first approached her. By July of 1893 she and Kelsey had enlisted one hundred members, who thereupon filed their Articles of Incorporation in Oakland and named themselves the Co-operative Brotherhood of Winters Island.[22]

The hundred, the maximum number stipulated in the articles, lived largely in the Bay area, although a scattering dwelt in other parts of the state: King City, Fresno, San Diego. Judging from those whose names and vocations were listed in the city directories, they were almost all skilled laborers. Perhaps the member most widely known to his contemporaries was A. J. Gregg, a carpenter of Alameda whom the Populist Party nominated for lieutenant-governor of the state in 1894.[23] Gregg served as first president of the brotherhood and as late as 1898 still managed the business affairs on the island.

Each new member expressed his belief in co-operation by signing the Articles of Incorporation and paying an initial fee of $1.25. Thereafter he was expected to pay the colony five dollars a month for one hundred months. In this way the brotherhood hoped to insure itself $6,000 annually for capital investment. In return each member received an equal share of the surplus revenues from the farm on Winters Island, all of the lands and improvements of which were to be held in common and worked co-operatively for the benefit of all. The corporation met quarterly and chose five directors; these five in turn selected officers from among themselves, appointed a superintendent, and designated those members who were actually to live and work upon the farm.

In 1896 the directors hired ten stockholders for operations on the island, but the number of residents was probably much higher. A picture of a picnic taken in the colony's barn on the Fourth of July, 1896, showed twenty-two men, women, and children.[24] The

[22]A MS copy of the Articles of Incorporation is in the files of the Secretary of State, Sacramento.

[23]He received 48,652 votes of 278,391 cast; *California Blue Book* (Sacramento, 1895), p. 255.   [24]San Francisco *Examiner*, August 16, 1896.

residents had much to do besides picnicking. In order to undergo any intensive agriculture, Winters Island had to be surrounded by levee, and much of the initial labor thus went for that purpose.

The dikes and the farm gradually took shape. Barns and houses rose. Of the island's 636 acres, purchased from Kelsey on liberal terms for $20,000, seventy were sown in hay, seventy in summer vegetables, and a few were planted in orchard. Onions proved one of the most successful crops.

Unfortunately the Co-operative Brotherhood of Winters Island was born coincident with the panic of 1893, and the depression years which followed sapped much of its infant vitality. Members who had glibly promised monthly payments began to find five dollars impressively large and increasingly hard to scrape together. By 1895 the membership rolls gaped with twenty vacancies, and most of the remaining brothers stood in arrears in payment. To save money the colony abandoned its plan to wall the entire land and drew its levee across the center of the island, leaving one half enclosed and one half for pasturage only.

Membership payments and the prices received for produce both fell consistently during 1894 and 1895, and, although the depression abated in the second half of the decade, the colony did not recover. A few resident members still shipped onions from the island as late as 1898 but with little enthusiasm. Exactly when the last colonists abandoned the site is not known, but by 1908 the 636 acres were owned by Mrs. Nevins alone.[25] She had purchased a decommissioned river boat, the *Orizaba*, and converted it to a lightship for the island. In 1930 at seventy-five years of age she still tended the beacon and watched the wild grasses encroaching like mist over the former lands of her Co-operative Brotherhood.

In the decade prior to the first World War a southern California irrigation engineer, William E. Smythe, began to maintain that any man could support himself and his family on a single acre of irrigated land. After Smythe delivered his first address in San

[25]*Official Map of Contra Costa County*, by T. A. McMahon, 1908; in State Library, Sacramento.

Diego on the subject, he received a letter: "Excuse me. I think you ought to be hanged. I am starving to death on 400 acres."[26] But many believed and followed Smythe, and he became the leader of a group of Californians calling themselves the Little Landers. In 1909 he established the first Little Landers Colony in the Tiajuana Valley, fourteen miles south of San Diego. The settlement, for which the colonists revived the name San Ysidro, claimed to demonstrate Smythe's premise that "a little land and a living, surely, is better than desperate struggle and wealth, possibly."[27]

William E. Smythe migrated from New England to California in successive steps through Nebraska and Idaho. His western experiences awakened within him a deep awareness of the importance and the problems of irrigation in connection with western settlement. He edited journals, initiated congresses, and pushed political measures on the subject. When he came to California early in the twentieth century, he found a region acutely conscious of its own land and water problems. In some areas immense holdings still remained in the hands of a few owners. In subdivided regions agricultural settlers paid dearly for irrigated land. Prices had been inflated by the excessive speculation of promoters who bought large tracts at low cost, installed a few utilities, and sold small plots for ridiculously high prices. The problem had become sufficiently serious by 1916 for the state legislature to appoint a commission on land colonization and rural credits and for the state university and the Commonwealth Club of California to co-operate in similar investigations. Shortly thereafter the state itself launched experiments in controlled colonization at Durham and Delhi, but with notable lack of success.

William Smythe, who participated in many of these researches, believed he had already solved the problem by establishing colonies in which future owners acted as their own subdividers. Large

---

[26]As quoted by William E. Smythe in Commonwealth Club of California, *Transactions*, XI (Dec., 1916), 425.

[27]Wm. E. Smythe, "Quest of the Fortunate Life," *West Coast Magazine*, XIII (June, 1913), 3.

stretches were purchased co-operatively, irrigated, and divided into small plots, the "little lands." For an initial $300 payment a colonist received a small town lot, an acre farm, and an interest in all public utilities. On his acre a man made a living and at the same time, because of the nearness of other colonists, enjoyed social and cultural advantages unknown in the average rural area. The colony in turn organized co-operative marketing so that the profits of the middle-man remained with the colony. Smythe established high ideals for his one-acre farmer,

a man who, if he be not in the city, is yet of the city . . . neither a farmer, nor a rancher, nor a trucker. He is a scientist. . . . He is an artist. . . . He is a man with initiative. . . . He is an independent, self-employing man. To his trees, his plants, and his vines he gives the ineffable touch of love . He is the spiritual man of the soil.[28]

About a dozen families answered Smythe's original call for recruits in 1909 and the first colony started with 120 acres of land a few miles south of San Diego. At the end of the year thirty-eight families had joined the Little Landers. By the fourth year the community had swelled to 116 families, 300 people in all, largely middle-aged or elderly.

Each family held only as much land as it could work without hiring additional help. This usually amounted to an acre, worked intensively, heavily fertilized, with diversified crops. One Little Lander, L. E. Scott, had left his position as shoemaker in Massachusetts to join San Ysidro at the age of sixty-three. From his plot he earned a net income of only a few dollars a month, but his food, fuel, light, water, laundry, and incidentals had been cared for and he had found status in a friendly circle of co-operative neighbors.

To aid the colonists in receiving full value for their product, the colony brought the producer as close as possible to the consumer. In the beginning a colonist in horse and buggy collected the day's output, and peddled the fruit and vegetables through the streets of San Diego. Later an auto truck did the same work, until finally an independent Little Lander's Co-operative Market was established on Sixth and B Streets in the heart of San Diego.

[28]San Francisco *Call*, Dec. 15, 1911, editorial page.

The colony's social life centered in a rude redwood clubhouse with two cobblestone fireplaces. Above the mantels shone mottoes from Walt Whitman: "I loaf and invite my soul" and "For the dear love of comrades." The clubhouse sheltered church sessions, gospel singing, regular Monday-night meetings of the colony, musical and literary programs, and night-school classes. This varied social program fulfilled Smythe's dictum: "Country life has failed on its spiritual side. . . . What is wanted is a form of country life that shall bring the people reasonably close to the great towns, both for market and social advantages; that shall give them near and numerous neighbors; that shall permit of the organization of a quick, rich, up-to-date social and intellectual life—full, elevating, satisfying."[29]

Smythe's message produced a state-wide movement. By 1916 at least four other Little Landers colonies had been organized and modeled roughly on the parent group at San Diego: Runnymede near Palo Alto; Hayward Heath in Alameda County; and colonies in the San Fernando Valley and at Cupertino near San Jose. They ranged in size from less than twenty families to over sixty. The colony at Runnymede required each settler to pass certain physical and financial tests and to pay for his farm in full on admission, and in similar ways the groups differed in details. They all agreed, however, on the fundamental proposition that a man could support his family on a piece of land no larger than that which he could work without hiring help.

The Little Landers movement disintegrated slowly as colonists found their holdings too small to be economically profitable and as more lucrative positions beckoned during the boom years of the first World War. One Little Lander indirectly accused Smythe of permitting "any dear, old lady with $500 or $600 to settle upon a stone pile . . . and try to make a living on it."[30] The exaggeration may conceal a kernel of truth for a large percentage of the San Ysidro colonists were elderly and many had had no agricultural experience. In January, 1915, a torrential flood ravaged the col-

[29] *West Coast Magazine*, XIII (June, 1913), 3.
[30] San Francisco *Examiner*, July 23, 1916.

ony and necessitated a relief fund to rush food, clothing, and bedding to the stricken settlement. But such discouragements only served to underscore the basic fact, observed by Professors M. S. Wildman and R. L. Adams in an investigation of 1916, that the Little Landers Colony at San Ysidro was unsound commercially and that one acre of land under those conditions was insufficient to provide a living for a family.[81]

These experiments in "handkerchief farming," as the newspapers labeled them, represented a reaction against increased urban congestion and an abortive attempt to return to the soil without sacrificing the advantages of the city. The Little Landers were utopian colonies because they withdrew from traditional society to incorporate a social message in concrete form. They did not, however, practice communal ownership of land or means of production or even communal housing and dining, so often associated with utopian life. Perhaps the Little Lander might be compared to a French peasant, attempting to wrest a modest living from a small piece of land. Actually he was seldom a farmer at all but rather a middle-aged or elderly Californian, a retired city dweller, seeking an easy and pleasant living for his declining years.

Mrs. Kate D. Buck, a dentist in Los Angeles, maintained, as did William E. Smythe, that a small plot of California soil within a co-operative colony promised relief from crowded cities and a new way of life. She organized the Los Angeles Fellowship Farms Company in 1912 and engaged the Rev. George E. Littlefield, who had established an earlier unsuccessful Fellowship Farms colony in Westwood, Massachusetts, in 1910, to choose a location and gather colonists for her scheme. In the winter of 1912-13 twelve families moved to the Farm, seventy-five acres lying northeast of Puente, each family receiving a tract slightly less than one acre and a share in the public utilities of the colony. Six central lots were reserved for communal activities. On the whole the pattern closely resembled the Little Landers at San Ysidro.

[81]Commonwealth Club, *Transactions,* XI (Dec., 1916), 382.

The membership never went beyond fifty or sixty, including a few eccentrics. The first secretary of the colony believed in nudism on highly idealistic grounds, allowed his three small boys to run naked, but never practiced his theories himself. A religious fanatic, William Brewer, vented his eccentricity by packing a bundle each weekend and hiking into Los Angeles to preach on Main Street.

Like the Little Landers colonies, Fellowship Farm disintegrated slowly as its members found the plots too small for profitable farming and, consequently, either left or bought larger pieces of adjacent property. With the end of equal land holdings, the co-operative spirit lost its meaning, and by 1926 the newly incorporated Maple Water Company assimilated its remaining assets, and Fellowship Farm ceased to exist.[32]

On February 18, 1915, Gerald Geraldson along with six comrades bared his arm to the surgeon at the Placer County Hospital. Seven members of the Army of Industry, a socialistic colony on the outskirts of Auburn, were giving live skin for a graft to an injured fellow member. The local newspapers headlined the incident[33] and thus brought to public attention an experiment in human relationships which for about a year had been expanding in preliminary form from the mind of Gerald Geraldson. The founder was a genuine humanitarian, a member of the active local Socialist Club, and the owner of a heavily mortgaged hundred-acre fruit ranch in the orchard districts west of Auburn. He believed that men could live together harmoniously if the thorn of private property were removed, and he looked to the establishment of a co-operative commonwealth of workingmen, self-sufficient, publicly owned, with every admitted citizen freely yielding all of his worldly goods to the community.

[32]I am indebted for information regarding Fellowship Farm to Miss Grace E. Buck, Henry Andrews, and Gilbert W. Wright of Puente, and Ardin D. Hotchkiss of Covina.

[33]Auburn *Journal,* Feb. 19, 1915. Newcastle *News,* Feb. 24, 1915.

Undoubtedly many of these ideas had developed from contact with the Kaweah Colony, for Geraldson had paid a total of forty-five dollars on a membership account to Kaweah between 1890 and 1892.[34] His social consciousness, however, dated from 1888 in San Francisco when Mrs. E. M. North, superintendent of schools, interested Geraldson, a young apprentice carpenter, in the Nationalism of Edward Bellamy. From that time, he says, "my main interest in life has been in that direction."[35] Gerald Geraldson returned to his father's ranch near Auburn in 1892, but his co-operative ideas did not blossom till October 14, 1914, when he sat down with twenty-five or thirty people and ate the first common meal at the Army of Industry on the old Geraldson farm.

Between 1914 and 1916 the ranch was considerably remodeled for its new undertaking. A packing plant was transformed into a communal dining hall; cottages were rendered more suitable for group living; and the general facilities of the fruit orchard were enlarged. Eventually the colony claimed ten buildings, half for living and half for work purposes.

Several of the local socialists in Auburn had traveled south to join the Llano Colony in 1914 and 1915. Those who remained, along with Wobblies, unemployed, and the generally discontented, provided the raw material for Geraldson's experiment. The initial membership of around thirty fluctuated widely during succeeding years, sometimes sinking to eight or ten but never exceeding forty. Admission was free. Geraldson felt that the Army of Industry should primarily aid those who had suffered from the world of private ownership, those "who had been crowded off the Property Band Wagon."[36] With experience, the colony increasingly emphasized this stipulation so that an individual's lack of property eventually became a requirement for admission. The community owned and provided everything — land, houses, furniture, clothes, and the means of production.

[34]Kaweah *Commonwealth* (weekly), Dec. 13, 1890; *ibid.* (monthly), Feb., 1892.
[35]Gerald Geraldson in letter to author, New York, Sept. 6, 1952.
[36]Gerald Geraldson in *Let's Go* (N.Y.), I (May, 1924), 1.

Geraldson and his followers welcomed with open arms any passing derelict. As a consequence, the Army was frequently beset with strangers imposing upon its good will in order to catch a little rest and a few good meals. Such impositions not only taxed the colony financially but often presented a poor impression to outsiders. M. B. Longmire, an ex-convict who had sought sanctuary at the colony for only a few days, later fell into trouble and was arrested in Auburn, while the local papers freely labeled him a member of the Army of Industry.[37] Many members did have police records, as may be guessed from an incident in which Geraldson tried to photograph the men working on the ranch and succeeded only in producing a rush to get out of the camera's range.

Certainly some members took advantage of the benevolent nature of Geraldson's experiment. The treasury allowed every man a few dollars for recreation in town on Saturday nights. After various episodes of drunkenness and brawling, the colony reduced the spending allotment, and to compensate themselves for the reduction some of the purported co-operators stole chickens and fruit from the colony's stores to sell in town. Surprising it is that Geraldson could subsequently write as charitably as he did regarding mankind:

Those of us who have survived have learned more about human nature than we ever thought existed. We see humans now just as lovable animals with a good deal of hair and primal instinct left and a very thin veneer of 'civilization', 'idealism', 'altruism', attached. Even those who have had 'the best opportunities' turn out to be utterly 'human' when this very thin covering is penetrated. And communal activity soon penetrates the covering.[38]

The questionable character of some of the members bred serious economic problems. Eventually for its own salvation, the colony withdrew questions of finance and buying and selling from the members and placed such decisions entirely in the hands of the executive. Members in meeting did, however, continue to elect

[37]Auburn *Journal*, July 2, 1915.
[38]Geraldson in *Let's Go,* I (May, 1924), 2.

supervisors of the various departments: a boss teamster, a boss orchardist, a boss cattleman. Each Monday morning after breakfast the supervisors met to allocate jobs for the week ahead, including the persistently difficult position of cook. The Army of Industry always complained of a high turnover in the kitchen.

Geraldson shared his basic ideas with most socialists of the day, but his conception of the sexes remained decidedly unorthodox. Woman, he believed, was responsible for "building up and conserving human values and promoting the Common Good,"[39] and should therefore be the sole influence on the rising generations. Man should be relegated to a secondary status, his chief functions to be labor and the fathering of children. His offspring, however, should be raised within "Mother Houses" in communal nurseries under the guidance of the women. Geraldson believed that such a system actually had existed in prehistoric societies and that the Original Sin had ushered in the rule of private property and the dominance of the male. His theories helped keep alive the local rumor that the Army of Industry housed the sexes separately and fostered free love. Lloyd Geraldson, the son of the founder, remembers in his school days having to bare his knuckles more than once in defense of the good name of his father's house.

The community lost money from the start. Geraldson himself covered the deficits in devotion to his cause. Whenever the opportunities arose, the more conscientious members took outside work and conveyed the earnings to the colony, as when a group cut fence posts and shakes in the Sierras one summer. When shipyards boomed in San Francisco during World War I, Geraldson and his son, Lloyd, moved to the Bay city, while Freeman Emerson, one of the most devoted and stable of the members, took charge of the colony. Geraldson hoped not only to recoup finances but to recruit co-operators in the shipyards.

The colony did not survive the war. Freeman Emerson, Arthur Z. Watkins, and a few others briefly carried on the venture, but its days in the field were numbered. By 1918 the Army of Industry

[39]Geraldson, "Production for Use," *Placer Herald* (Auburn), May 11, 1940.

in Auburn had surrendered to private property and ceased its battle for the co-operative commonwealth. Geraldson, having found few new members in San Francisco, returned to Auburn believing that for success a utopian colony required harder economic conditions than life in California provided. Partly for this reason and partly hoping to secure financial support for the revival and expansion of his ideas, in 1922 he left his family and crossed the continent to New York City. Although failing in his quest for capital, he devoted his idealistic energies to settlement work on the East Side and still today looks upon his Brotherhood House in New York as the potential nucleus of a co-operative community which will eventually realize the ideals of the Army of Industry.

Years before Gerald Geraldson opened his settlement house in New York, "Father" Finis E. Yoakum had founded and fostered a similar mission in Los Angeles to feed the hungry, care for the destitute, and preach the Gospel to the needy. By 1914 his efforts embraced the Pisgah Home where the distressed received food and lodging, the Pisgah Ark in the Arroyo Seco which housed and attempted to reform delinquent girls, a store nearby which handled donated goods, and Pisgah Gardens in the San Fernando Valley for tuberculosis, cancer, and mental cases. In this year Finis Yoakum conceived yet another branch to the Lord's Kingdom — a community isolated from the city and modeled on a pattern of religious and social dedication.

For this purpose he purchased 3,200 acres in the valleys and mountains north and east of Santa Susana along the Los Angeles-Ventura county line. Dr. Yoakum called his new colony Pisgah Grande, and his followers constructed a two-story headquarters, individual dwellings, a communal dining hall, a schoolhouse, a post office, a watchtower with a constant flame for eternal vigil and prayer—all set in a new Canaan with prosperous gardens, goats' milk, and honey. Most of the resident colonists came from the mission in Los Angeles, but a few from more established ranks of society found at Pisgah Grande an agreeable escape from city and competition. By the time Father Yoakum died in August, 1920, seventy-five members lived at the colony.

Even before "Daddy" Yoakum's decease, charges of scandal and a grand jury investigation into unsanitary conditions robbed Pisgah Grande of much of its former enthusiasm. The two sons of Dr. Yoakum and the long-time manager at the colony, James Cheek, tried to perpetuate the founder's dream after his death, but the community slowly crumbled, leaving only broken and ghostly buildings which still stand in an isolated valley of the Santa Susana Mountains.[40]

Stephen Rozum, a philosophical Pole ruminating over his youthful troubles, considered that most of them stemmed from his inquisitive nature. In Poland while studying for the priesthood, he had questioned the Roman Catholic hierarchy and had consequently been dismissed from the seminary. Following his emigration to the United States in 1906, he had worked his way across the continent as a waiter. In San Francisco he developed an interest in Hinduism which led him into a monastery of the Vedanta Society. Again he asked too many questions and was expelled. Walking one day up Market Street in San Francisco he heard a street-corner orator describing the true path to the world's salvation. It was the message of William E. Riker, "Father" to a small, growing band of disciples. Stephen Rozum heard the word with delight; his questions were answered; he had found his spiritual home.

Father Riker called his promulgation the Perfect Christian Divine Way, and he was ready to lead his followers to a utopian colony, a Holy City which would embody the world's most perfect government. He himself was a native Californian, born in

[40]I am indebted to Mr. Martin Litton of the Los Angeles *Times* for much groundwork in uncovering details of Pisgah. An article of his appeared in the *Times* for July 6, 1952. He was also kind enough to allow me access to the files of the *Times* which contain clippings, memos, copies of letters, and an unpublished MS, "Pisgah Home," signed "H.C.D." James Cheek, former manager at Pisgah Grande, has been kind enough to read critically this section and offer suggestions.

Oakdale in 1873, who spent his young life in Oroville where he attended the public schools to the third or fourth grade. Later he became a mechanic and moved to San Francisco at the age of nineteen.

Riker had always been deeply interested in magic and spiritualism; he had been what Rozum called a "searcher" from childhood. By 1918 he had experienced various divine manifestations, including an earthquake on the occasion of the first preachment of the P.C.D.W. Rather than through Divine Breath like Thomas Lake Harris, Riker, "the Comforter," received messages from God by means of his nerves. "The Philosophy of the Comforter and the Author, is the entire product of his Nerves, without any Book Learning. It is also 100 percent brand new, all-wise and strictly up-to-date."[41] Basic to most of his ideas was a racism suggestive of the Ku Klux Klan. Fond of metaphor, he assigned positions corresponding to parts of the human body to the ethnic groupings of mankind: the head for the Jews, the trunk for the Gentiles, the arms for the yellow races, and the legs for the black. The white race was meant to direct mankind; all others, merely to serve. The breaking of this God-sent law by miscegenation or the loosening of the cords of segregation constituted race murder, releasing disease and dreadful evil. Thus Riker could describe the Fair Employment Practices Commission as a scheme "to get the negroes and orientals [sic] votes through their devilish promise and proposal of putting over that F. E. P. race crime doctrine plan, that will 100 per cent sell the great White race people down the river into mulish human pollution and defeat."[42]

Riker aspired politically and, in his four campaigns for governor of California, he proposed that all Negroes and Asiatics be denied the right to own or run businesses in the state and that they be relegated to their proper station of serving the white race.[43] On the day of Armageddon, he prophesied, California

[41][William E. Riker,] *The Philopsohy of the Nerves Revealed* (Holy City, Calif., n.d.), Cover.

[42]Riker, *World Peace and How to Have It* (Holy City, n.d.), p. 5.

[43]Handbills Recommending Wm. E. Riker for Governor of Calif., 1940; Huntington Library.

will be struck by earthquakes which will consume all men except Jews and Gentiles, the royal family of earth.

In 1918 Riker purchased a few acres in the Santa Cruz mountains midway between San Jose and Santa Cruz. Here in a high, quiet valley bordering the state highway amid hills forested with redwoods, he created Holy City. Thirty of his followers, including Stephen Rozum and David Aaron, a Jewish disciple, moved south to the new Zion and within a few years had built cabins, a garage and service station, a grocery store, and a restaurant.[44] Located near the summit of a mountain road, they profited by a sizable trade from passing automobiles, attracting attention with huge primitive paintings and caustic quotations spread over the fronts of the buildings.

The land, which eventually embraced two hundred acres, belonged to the community in Riker's name. The colony supplied housing, furniture, clothes, and all the means of production but engaged in only the most rudimentary agriculture, concentrating on trade and mechanics. It opened a barber shop and an extensive print shop in addition to its garage and store and restaurant. Members received no wages beyond the satisfaction of their needs at community expense. Although the group met occasionally to discuss policies, the government of the colony was carefully controlled by Riker.

Members were unmarried and living quarters were strictly segregated by sexes. As in a Shaker colony, no children were born and no one was particularly concerned about the perpetuation of the community. Holy City placed itself and its cause in the hands of destiny.

While still in San Francisco, Riker had published a small monthly paper called the *Enlightener* in which he indulged freely his penchant for the parable and the metaphor; but no regular journal appeared at Holy City. The print shop at the colony did produce, however, numerous pamphlets and handbills which were

---

[44]Eugene T. Sawyer, *History of Santa Clara County, Calif.* (Los Angeles, 1922), p. 1553.

distributed freely to visitors and throughout the state during the political campaigns of the Comforter.

Newspapers in the outer world, especially those of San Francisco, reported every escapade of Riker's turbulent life, freely emphasizing the sensational aspects. Grist was seldom lacking for their mills. At one time or another the courts ordered Riker to answer charges of reckless driving, fraud, evasion of taxation, breach of promise, sedition, and murder. Acquitted in all cases, Father Riker was able to boast that he "never lost a battle," and even the blatant press accounts of the trials swelled the trade from Sunday drivers at Holy City.

Perhaps due to Riker's increasing notoriety in court and press, by 1952 the number of members at Holy City had dwindled to twelve. These stalwarts had all been a part of the original band which had followed Riker from San Francisco more than thirty years earlier. They now averaged nearly sixty years, and Riker himself was seventy-nine. Some received old-age pensions from the government, checks which helped the community treasury remain solvent. A hired cook supervised the communal dining hall, but on the whole the needs of these oldsters caused little expense. Some of the stores, the garage, and the service station had been rented and the income enabled the colony to maintain its proud policy of no donations. Stephen Rozum continued to run the print shop and a large proportion of his work came from the outer world, netting the colony another small source of profit. Rozum, now sixty-eight, when asked what he envisioned in the future for the colony, quietly answered, "Holy City belongs to mankind and mankind never dies."

Stretching north from the banks of the Tuolumne River southwest of Modesto, about sixty miles from Holy City, lie the 155 acres of Tuolumne Co-operative Farms. Herds of over thirty milking cows and seventy goats, fields of tall alfalfa and corn, with walnut and pomegranate trees along the road, lend a prosperous color. A small central group of buildings, somewhat in need of paint, provides housing, barns, and storehouses for the colony.

Tuolumne Farms is but one experiment in community life stemming from the pacifist thought of a nebulous number of Californians, including many Quakers. These sincere idealists are deeply concerned with the increasing militarism and materialism of American life. In order to raise their children in a more peaceful and spiritual atmosphere, some have moved to rural areas and others have abandoned the United States entirely, settling in western Canada or in Costa Rica. They have experimented with community forms ranging from the Fellowship Council in the town of Tracy, a loose "extension of neighborliness"[45] in which a group of families co-operates in various ways, to the more tightly knit colony at Tuolumne Farms.

Four families conceived the Modesto project in 1946, hoping to develop a farming community where individuals could "grow more mature in all their relations with others."[46] They also desired to incorporate some of the more universal features of the Danish Folk School, a Scandinavian scheme wherein small communities of students and teachers study humanism primarily through discussions and everyday life. Like the Folk School, students at Tuolumne Farms came for varying lengths of time; but, unlike the Scandinavian precedent, the student could elect to make the colony his permanent home. After passing a six-month trial, he could pay a $100 fee and become a full-fledged member. The number of residents has not been large: nine adults and eight children being the maximum at any one time, with a turnover of about fifty per cent during the six years of co-operative existence.

The community owns the 155 acres of land, the four houses, and all means of production. Workers receive a salary which varies with needs; the more children, for example, the higher the wage. The families dine separately in their own houses and the bachelors rotate for meals among them. The combined membership meets monthly for business and weekly for work assignments.

[45]A phrase used by one of its founders, Robert Boyd, in interview with author, June 6, 1952.

[46]George Burleson, member of Tuolumne Farms, in letter to author, July 24, 1952.

The large turnover in members would seem to indicate the failure of the colony to satisfy material or spiritual expectations. None of the four founding families is still resident. Yet the Farm has been maintained and shows signs of successful continuance. Perhaps its greatest strength lies in its desire to develop and to experiment with new ideas, an approach which the colony would claim as a highly desirable background for family life.

With these smaller groups, the problems of accurately defining a utopian colony become glaringly evident. Categories fail and borderlines grow hazy in trying to isolate common denominators for such varied experiments as Pisgah Grande and the Army of Industry. Could the rationality of Tuolumne Farms have anything in common with the emotionalism of Holy City? Many of these communities, like Joyful and Modjeska's colony, involved very few people and existed for less than a year. Others, like Winters Island and Fellowship Farm, left only a meager record. The significance of two colonies lies more logically in other fields than in the utopian story: the Mormons at San Bernardino whose rise and fall measured Utah policy rather than local failure, and the Little Landers whose methods of land settlement almost eclipsed their social and utopian aspects. Somewhere, however, the lines must be drawn, and regardless of their differences, all of these kaleidoscopic colonies have reflected a vision of the ideal state, all have withdrawn from traditional society of which they disapproved, and all have offered to their former culture a new social pattern as a means of salvation.

CHAPTER 9

Utopian Colonies in California

REVIEWING the collection of seemingly dissimilar histories which appears in the foregoing pages, what generalizations can we draw? Do any broad conclusions emerge, or is this volume merely a series of disconnected episodes? The communities all existed within the boundaries of a single political entity, California, and they qualified as utopian colonies because they attempted to establish a new pattern of society after their withdrawal from the old. It may well be asked, however, what broader American trends of thought they as a group shared or reflected. Why did they so seldom hold together? What aspects of failure were common to all? And how did the collapse of a utopia affect the particular utopians involved?

One question which naturally arises is the relation of these colonies to other American communitarian movements, such as that imported by Robert Owen in the 1820's. Although widespread and important in its time, Owenism filtered little into the later California period. Occasionally the utopian newspapers quoted Robert Owen, but usually relegated him to a filler position. No characteristically Owenite terms, such as "parallelogram," ever arose in planning the communities. No attempts at economic co-operation between congenial colonies, similar to Owen's "villages of co-operation," ever materialized. The Altrurian colonists by their reorganization of June, 1895, hoped to create a series of economically co-operating units, but their supply of money and morale had by then too far diminished for success. Cyrus Teed in 1892 presented Thomas Lake Harris with a scheme to unite several colonies,[1] but Harris politely refused, and Teed found no other supporters for his idea.

If Harris was not an Owenite, he was, nevertheless, deeply influenced by Fourierism. Harris spent his early youth in New York State during the 1840's and 1850's, the palmiest of Fourierist decades, and his later congregation in New York City included Horace Greeley of the New York *Tribune* who at the time was a leading exponent of Fourierism. Harris claimed to have guided Greeley into various philanthropic enterprises, and, conversely, he probably learned much about Fourierism from the editor. Similarities with Fourierist ideas emerged frequently in Harris' writings, as, for example, when he prophesied a great industrial army welded together by the "power of solidarity," in which men would be divided into bands, bands into series, and series into regiments.[2] The words as well as the ideas in this passage are distinctly Fourieristic. Some of Harris' cosmic interpretations indicated a further acquaintance with Fourier, as when he spoke of Mercury as "a Phalansterian world" and pictured interplanetary relationships much as Fourier had described the marriage of planets in the scheme of creation.[3]

Harris, however, was the only California utopian deeply influenced by Fourier. The Altrurian freedom in allowing the colonist to choose his own job suggested the Fourierist goal of attractive labor with individual choice and frequent rotation. But no colony possessed a genuine Fourieristic phalanstère or resembled a true phalanx in any great detail.

Since Henry George's *Progress and Poverty* appeared in 1879 and was widely read just prior to the inauguration of Icaria Speranza, Joyful, Kaweah, Winters Island, and Altruria, it would

[1]San Francisco *Chronicle*, Feb. 26, 1892.

[2]"Glimpses of Social and Sexual Order" (n.d., unpublished typescript in T. L. Harris Collection, Columbia University Library), p. 2.

[3]*Arcana of Christianity* (3 vols., N.Y., 1858-67), I, 69; as quoted in Schneider, p. 30.

not be surprising to discover a single-tax colony in California; but none appeared. William E. Smythe reflected the influence of Henry George by proclaiming that the increased value of land should accrue to the community as a whole,[4] but Smythe's Little Landers did not follow George's revenue ideas. Although the single-tax movement did produce a few colony experiments— notably Fairhope, Alabama, in 1894—it did not primarily point toward reforms through the communitarian approach. Most of the members of California colonies, especially at Kaweah, Altruria, and Llano, were well versed in George's theories, especially in the advantages of meeting all costs of government by one tax based on the appreciating value of land. Their newspapers frequently discussed the single tax, only to reject it, however, as a partial and superficial remedy for the ills of the world.[5]

Edward Bellamy's Nationalism, the movement of the late 1880's and early 1890's looking toward a fully nationalized, co-operative state, struck a more sympathetic chord in the California colonies than any other nation-wide impulse. We have already observed the extent to which Nationalism interrelated with Theosophy. Kaweah revered *Looking Backward* as the "Bible of the present"[6] and drew a large proportion of its members from Nationalist ranks. Thomas Lake Harris looked upon Nationalism as a movement congenial to his own, only protesting Bellamy's lack of a religious foundation. Gerald Geraldson considered Bellamy the inspiration for a lifetime of social consciousness. Nationalism played a dominant influence in the founding of Altruria, and though Llano itself was born too late for direct contact, its founder, Job Harriman, had been associated with Nationalist clubs in San Francisco during the 1890's and carried many of their concepts into his later work. Indeed, the first California Nationalist

[4]Smythe, "Quest of the Fortunate Life," *West Coast Magazine*, XIII (June, 1913), 3.

[5]*Altrurian*, Nov. 22, 1894. *Western Comrade*, II (Sept., 1914), 24-25. *La Jeune Icarie*, Aug.-Sept., 1880. Laurence Gronlund, *Co-operative Commonwealth* (Boston, 1884), p. 86.

[6]*Commonwealth*, March 1, 1890.

Convention, convening in San Francisco on April 8, 1890, included among its delegates numerous former and future utopians: Burnette Haskell leading a large deputation of Kaweahans, Erastus Kelsey and Eugene Hough later of Winters Island, and Job Harriman of the future Llano. All of the colonies found appealing aspects in the Bellamy message, in such basic ideas as the demoralizing effects of a competitive economy and the advantages of the co-operative way of life. They looked with favor on Bellamy's conclusion that the means of production should be controlled by the people as a whole and that human nature will respond to the improvement of its environment.

A less pervasive, but nevertheless significant, influence on the late nineteenth-century colonies was the work of Laurence Gronlund. His *Co-operative Commonwealth*, an exposition of Marxism adapted to the American environment, directly inspired and guided Kaweah, even providing a model for some of its institutions, such as the time-check. Thomas Lake Harris at Fountain Grove and Edward Payne at Altruria both read Gronlund enthusiastically.

The works of Bellamy and Gronlund most frequently attracted the laboring man, and, for the same reasons, labor unions in turn often nurtured the California utopias. Kaweah and Llano grew directly out of union activity; Icaria, Altruria, and the Army of Industry accepted labor support; and Thomas Lake Harris expressed interest and sympathy in labor organizations, though he relied but little on them for recruits. The co-operative strain which ran through the early history of the labor movement, through the National Labor Union, the Grange, and especially the Knights of Labor,[7] undoubtedly influenced Haskell and probably Harriman, Payne, and most of those who entered utopianism from the labor fold. As an organizer for the Farmers' Alliance, Mrs. Kate Lockwood Nevins must surely have carried the Alliance's co-operative ideas into her planning of Winters Island. It may well be that Kaweah, emerging from San Francisco in the

[7]Chester M. Destler, *American Radicalism* (New London, Conn., 1946), pp. 9-10.

1880's, and Llano, from Los Angeles in 1914, were products of identical stages of labor agitation. Kaweah preceded Llano simply because San Francisco labor had achieved a coherence in the eighties which Los Angeles workingmen could not claim till the decade before the first World War.

The labor movement in San Francisco and Los Angeles was frequently allied with socialism both as a political party and as an ideal, and socialism often stimulated the founding of the California colonies. It influenced the formation of Llano, the Army of Industry, Kaweah, Altruria, and Icaria Speranza. This mainspring, however, was not Marxism, which regarded community experiments as superficial and naive. By the late nineteenth century, Marxism, at least in the sense of economic determinism, had penetrated all socialist thought, but the question of the class struggle continued to differentiate sharply the Marxist of the International from the communitarian socialist. Most of the leaders of California utopianism, with the possible exceptions of Haskell and Harriman, denied the class struggle as a necessary element in reform. Burnette Haskell, as we have seen, shared many ideas with both the Black International of Anarchism and the Red International of Marxism, but his thought patterns had evolved more directly from less class-conscious Americans like Edward Bellamy and Laurence Gronlund. Job Harriman, perhaps the most class-conscious of all the California utopian leaders, repudiated later in his life his earlier stand on this subject and concluded that the economically fortunate were often best suited to advance the cause of the co-operative commonwealth.[8]

Since the religious colonies, such as Fountain Grove and Point Loma, drew on the secular thought currents associated with Nationalism and socialism, and since the secular colonies proclaimed the brotherhood of man so often as to make it a semi-religious sanction, it may be wondered how fundamental the differences between the religious and secular patterns really were. Certainly the secular colonies came close to religious zeal in pro-

---

[8] In Preface to E. S. Wooster, *Communities of the Past and Present*, pp. v-vi.

claiming their new way of life. Nevertheless, the two utopian categories represented widely divergent ideas, especially in their concepts of man and his environment. In the establishment of a better world the secular colonies attacked the environment; the religious colonies, the individual. Since man is the product of his nurture and breeding, said the secularist, and since he has been molded into an antagonistic and competitive beast by his culture, any hope for improvement must come from an initial change in the society which has made man what he is. In the words of Burnette Haskell, "selfish nature was but the product of conditions, and . . . when these were altered human disposition would change."[9] The religious colonist replied that the revision of society will remain fruitless as long as man himself continues in his present unregenerate state. Once man is refined, the institutions and culture of which he is a part will automatically improve. In the secular groups the communism of the community was an end in itself; in the religious, only an expedient for the regeneration of mankind. Both sought the attainment of brotherhood, but one required brotherhood to usher in a better world while the other demanded a new society in order to achieve brotherhood.

For any utopian, religious or secular, politics provided no springboard for reform; by his withdrawal from society he tacitly admitted the impossibility of reformation by conventional legislative means. Not that the secular colonist would have eschewed the political arena could he have controlled it; herein he differed again from his religious counterpart, who saw in politics no hope whatever.

Perfectionism lay at the heart of California utopianism just as it has in most patterns of utopian thought. Man's moral character can be perfected, the colonist believed, and the attempt to do so was the supreme ethical good. Fountain Grove, the Theosophical colonies, and Pisgah stressed the spiritual perfection, but all—religious and secular alike—agreed that man can achieve in this life not only freedom from sin, but the highest of the virtues,

[9]"Kaweah," Out West, XVII (Sept., 1902), 303.

truth, beauty, goodness. And society itself, like man, can be perfectly remolded. In this sense, utopians were also millenarians looking for the coming of the ideal commonwealth and eternal happiness on this earth. Critics of the static aspects of utopianism have often had this millennialism in mind. Arnold Toynbee sees utopian movements as attempts to peg progress at a given future point wherein all subsequent change will be unnecessary.[10] David Starr Jordan, while president of Stanford University, emphasized the same idea by referring to utopian colonies as unchanging societies in a condition of arrested development.[11] Even Marxism, forswearing utopianism as it does, reflects an element of static millennialism, or at least a disinclination to predict further progress after the millennial, classless society has been achieved. Certainly an air of stagnation pervades most of the literary utopias, as for example, in *The Republic* where every individual is pigeonholed by the age of thirty with no possibility of deviation thereafter. In such a society change could come rarely and probably then only as revolution.

Commentators notwithstanding, the static nature of utopian thought is notably missing from the California colonies. Probably the criticism of Toynbee and Jordan springs from too great an acquaintance with the literary utopias and too little with the practical ventures. At any rate, the California colonies, especially the secular, approached their task tentatively. We will start with this system, they said, but let our General Assembly have full power to change continually as we go along. In Harriman's words:

Whoever thoughtfully lives in a community and adjusts himself to its life and growing needs, must learn that at best any theory or viewpoint or supposed fact can serve only as [a] working hypothesis, a point from which to start for a new goal.[12]

If the California colonists shared a perfectionist ideal with

[10]*A Study of History*, abr. of Vols. I-VI by D. C. Somervell (N.Y., 1946), pp. 183, 431-32.

[11]*The Care and Culture of Men* (San Francisco, 1896), p. 230.

[12]In Preface to Wooster, *Communities*, p. x.

utopians elsewhere, they also reflected in common an attitude of escapism, a desire to forget the society they had known and to start fresh. From what did a man seek to escape when he founded or joined a utopian colony on the Mojave Desert, on timbered foothills, or in some sheltered canyon of Sonoma County? Primarily he fled insecurity. The colony promised him and his family food and shelter, a job, education for his children, and care in his old age. It promised him relief from the ravages of depression or from the specter of future depression. Harrisites went further, predicting that "there is no end possible to this immeasurable torture . . . of the long-suffering race here below" except in the communal approach of Harris.[13] The majority of the Kaweah colonists joined, according to Haskell, "to escape the grind and worry of the outside world, to secure social advantages and harmonious surroundings."[14]

The drive for release from insecurity was intensified, of course, by industrialism. Not that the California colonies sprang from slums and heavy industry; the influence was not that direct. But a surprising number of leaders and founders had experienced the pronounced evils of industrial conditions: Thomas Lake Harris in London and Manchester; Katherine Tingley on the East Side of New York; Burnette Haskell and Job Harriman with labor unions, logical extensions of industrial activity; Gerald Geraldson and Finis Yoakum with settlement houses in the crowded areas of large cities. Certainly California prior to the first World War knew no festering centers of industrial discontent but only a weak and inchoate urban industrialism.[15] Yet it is not heavy manufacturing that produces utopianism. Industrialism which weighs oppressively on the laborer is more apt to kindle a harsh social criticism and to sharpen class antagonisms. Utopianism springs more char-

[13]Arthur A. Cuthbert, *Life and World-work of Thomas Lake Harris* (Glasgow, 1909), p. 80.

[14]"Kaweah," *Out West*, XVII (Sept., 1902), 316.

[15]Frank L. Kidner, *California Business Cycles* (Berkeley, 1946), pp. 15, 20, shows the percentage of California population engaged in manufacturing rising at a slow pace from 17% in 1870 to about 25% in 1930, a low figure compared with about 30% in the U.S. as a whole.

acteristically from periods of less acrid social judgment, when the
class struggle is not emphasized. Thus, Robert Owen appeared
in early nineteenth-century England; French utopian socialism
arose in the period from 1820 to 1840; and the highest incidence
of utopianism east of the Mississippi occurred in the 1840's and
1850's. In this connection it is interesting to note that the greatest
number of utopian colonies in California existed during the years
of the first World War.

In any case, many a man joined a colony with the idea of
exchanging city life for an escape into the country. The propaganda pamphlets for Altruria, Kaweah, and Llano persistently
painted the beauties and healthfulness of their rural environs. The
Little Landers sought to preserve the social and cultural advantages of city life but only after fleeing urban congestion. Along
with the city, the utopian hoped to extricate himself from the
complex coils of modern capitalist society. He was the frustrated
and disappointed driftwood tossed up by the competitive sea.
He had run afoul of the profit motive, had known the resulting
contentious psychology, and feared the corruption of himself
and his children. The bitter resentment of the profit motive surged
like a persistent current through the utopian newspapers and
literature. Though all colonists had not failed economically or
socially, they had uniformly lost faith in the ends which external
society had set. In this sense utopian colonies could be regarded
as protests against the establishment of frequently unattainable
goals. The competitive scheme expects every individual, like
Horatio Alger, to reach the top. The social and personal consequences of failure to attain such a goal have produced many a
captious critic of that society and many a utopian colonist.

Each colony had a goodly number of social misfits, as the
leaders realized too well. Haskell and Wooster, along with most
secular colonists, frankly admitted idiosyncrasies among their
comrades; and the religious colonies, although usually refraining
from discussion of their aberrant members, clearly had their share.
One may wonder whether any new social order could succeed
when burdened with the misfits and eccentrics of the old.

Deep in the psychology of most colonists undoubtedly welled a desire for identity with a strong integral community. Modern urban centers, like certain frontier areas, minimize, if not totally destroy, the feeling of inclusion and participation in a community. A small, unified colony fulfilled the desire to belong, to feel needed, counteracting the intense loneliness which modern man so often suffers in the midst of a city population.

But if the escapist is one who by nature tends to flee from difficult situations, his refuge in a utopian colony was an unfortunate choice. As Harriman said, "Under a system of private ownership of property one may exclude from his thought and companionship whomsoever he may dislike; . . . in a co-operative community this cannot be done."[16] Harriman believed that this forced contact with unwelcome neighbors was a stimulus to intellectual growth in the co-operative colony, but he might also have noted that it was one of the annoying sources of conflict. Thus the paradox of isolation in a crowd became further intensified when the individual, surrounded by dissension, failed to assuage his loneliness within the new community. He then often came to the point which Haskell reached when he "longed again for the large city, where one's next door neighbor is unknown."[17]

To assign general causes of failure can be dangerously misleading, for every colony faced different circumstances, a different membership, and different leaders. But certain indications appear consistently enough to warrant selection as common causes of collapse. In the area of political contributions to failure, the distinction between the religious and the secular colonies takes on unusual significance. The average life of religious colonies in California has been over twenty years, while that of the secular colonies has been well under ten. Most analysts of utopian experiments, from Charles Nordhoff to Arthur Bestor, Jr., have observed this discrepancy between the life spans of the sectarian and the secular and, therefore, have concluded that religious fer-

---

[16]In Wooster, *Communities*, p. viii.
[17]"Kaweah," *Out West*, XVII (Sept., 1902), 318.

vor is one of the ingredients requisite to colony longevity. It would be hard to show, however, that the religious colonist evidenced any greater zeal in the pursuit of his belief than his secular relative, who often transmuted temporal ideals into a spiritual ardor.

The essential distinction lay not in religious faith but in a rational or irrational attitude and the corresponding reflections in political life. The sectarian colonies placed little confidence in reason, emphasizing revelation and unquestioning obedience to a religious leader. From these suppositions an autocratic government usually sprang. The secular colonies on the other hand, proudly pointed to the rationality of their approach and in theory endowed every man with sufficient reason to criticize the authority under which he lived. As a result, extremely democratic institutions, usually culminating in a sovereign general assembly, characterized the secular colonies. And it is precisely in these general assemblies, conferring on every man the right to speak his mind freely, that tremendous conflicts arose. The minute books of Icaria and Kaweah and the newspapers of Llano and Altruria related interminable sessions airing personal disputes, questioning minor administrative decisions, or seeking individual dispensations. Ernest Wooster might have been referring to all secular utopias when he dubbed Llano "democracy with the lid off."[18]

The rationality of the secular approach thus produced dissension which usually proved quickly fatal. This does not imply that rational democracy must necessarily fail. But in the absence of other conditions—social control by a judiciary, economic stability, time to solidify new cultural habits—the rational approach of the secular colony inserted an obstacle which seldom confronted the religious group at all.

The social causes of failure were closely allied to the political. In the screening of new members all colonies met a stumbling block, but the secular groups had the severest problem. The religious colony required unquestioning acceptance of leadership,

18"They Shared Equally," *Sunset*, LIII (July, 1924), 81.

and a member who so capitulated rarely caused dissension; if he did, the leader could eject him with no questions and little disturbance. The secular colony usually required agreement with a statement of principles or a pledge as a condition of membership. But the pledge did not abrogate the right to criticize, and once admitted, the member could be dissociated only by action of the general assembly and usually a nine-tenths or unanimous vote. The power of dismissal provided the general assemblies with additional venom in the airing of personal quarrels and disputes.

It may be wondered that the colonies in California did not establish sufficient social controls to mitigate personal dissension. In the religious colonies, such control could be exerted by the leader, and a word from Katherine Tingley or Thomas Lake Harris was usually enough to correct a quarrelsome attitude. In the secular colonies the pressure of public opinion might have been sufficient if it had been effectively channeled, as in sessions of "mutual criticism," a method successfully used in the earlier colonies of Oneida in New York and Amana in Iowa. Kaweah projected a judiciary with a Court of Private Disputes, a Court of Public Disputes, and a Court of Prizes and Awards, but the scheme did not materialize. No courts other than the assemblies were provided in any of the colonies, and consequently the general meetings wasted in personal quarrels time badly needed for decisions of policy and administration.

Victor Calverton believes that the basic cause of failure in utopian experiments has been their agrarian nature in conflict with an industrial age.[19] Admittedly the California colonies were agrarian, but even in an industrial era an agrarian settlement can succeed provided it owns enough land to produce a staple crop. Fountain Grove established a staple product and the importance of its wine can hardly be overestimated as a factor in its longevity. However, no other California colony, with the possible exception of Icaria Speranza, created a sound basis for trade by successfully concentrating on a staple. The avocados at Point Loma were not

[19]*Where Angels Dared to Tread* (Indianapolis, 1941), p. 366.

produced on a sufficiently large scale, the alfalfa and pears at
Llano could not easily be transported to market, and the supply
of cut timber at Kaweah never greatly exceeded home consumption. As a rule, the colonies varied their efforts, at least during
the initial years, in order to establish a well-rounded and self-
sufficient economy. This attempt stemmed logically from the
concept of withdrawal, for economic independence, it was
thought, smoothed the road to social independence. The theory
proved unfortunate, for the colonies were too small to transcend
the laws of the economy with which they were surrounded. Since
the division of labor vitally supports the modern economy, the
colonies could well have used a staple in order to engage in that
division and its resulting exchanges. It was not necessary that they
devote themselves to industrial production, but it would have
been distinctly to their economic advantage to take part in the
external exchange and division of labor. Geraldson quite correctly
referred to the Army of Industry as "an embryo in the womb of
Mother Property, [which] for a considerable period must draw
its support from her body."[20]

In the realization of a staple crop, or, for that matter, in the
erection of any kind of sound economy, the colonies suffered
from lack of capital. Often, where treasuries furnished adequate
sums, the money was used for purposes other than the creation
of a settled economy. Fountain Grove and Point Loma drew on
sufficient resources from the beginning because both had wealthy
donors. They dissipated their capital, however, in unnecessarily
ornate buildings or elaborate printing projects from which ac-
crued no material gain. The economic success of the Mormons
at San Bernardino may be largely attributed to their ability to
command capital on the personal credit of Lyman and Rich. The
Army of Industry, on the other hand, struggled under a heavy
mortgage, and the pressure from the mortgagee to "cease this
socialist nonsense" and rent to Japanese tenants contributed to
Geraldson's final submission. Neither Altruria, Icaria Speranza,

[20]In a letter to the author, Sept. 6, 1952.

Kaweah, nor Llano, relying as they did on membership fees and small donations, had sufficient capital to tide them over the early, less productive years.

No clear causal relationship can be observed between periods of general depression and either the founding or the failure of the California colonies. Comparing the dates of six colonies (Kaweah, Winters Island, Altruria, Llano, the Army of Industry, and Holy City—those which were initiated in California, not in another part of the country with a later extension to California) with one of Wesley C. Mitchell's charts of business cycles, all of the six colonies grew out of depression conditions.[21] But if we turn to a table in Mitchell (p. 335) showing the crests and troughs of the business cycle, we find that for the same group of colonies three were born at the crest of a business cycle and three in a trough. In short, it cannot be shown that economic depressions directly caused utopian movements in California. Nor can it be concluded that the failures were necessarily associated with depressions. The reduced business activity following the panic of 1893 profoundly affected Winters Island, and the Theosophists at Point Loma suffered catastrophically after 1930; but prosperity has also undermined utopia. Members abandoned both Llano and the Army of Industry when attracted by boom wages during the first World War. The fear of depression did, of course, stimulate the desire for security, but the actual conditions of depression or prosperity were widely variable factors in the inception or failure of the colonies.

From the standpoint of the individual, the utopias miscarried because their members could not sacrifice consistently to the common good. Authoritarian control within the religious colonies could force the individual into self-denial for a longer period than he would otherwise endure, but within most colonists, in spite of or because of repression, the strain in the end became too great. It may be said that the failure of long-term altruism without authoritarian control has been a characteristic of American society

[21]Mitchell, *Business Cycles* (N.Y., 1927), pp. 368-69.

—if not all societies—from the beginning, that Jamestown and Plymouth and New Harmony all learned the fact, and that the incessant breakdown of good will reflects an innate human disposition against excessive co-operation.

Such a conclusion ignores the flexibility of human nature and its protean quality relative to the culture which produces it. A competitive milieu will evoke a competitive man, and conversely, as Margaret Mead has shown with the Zuñi Indians. With them the co-operative person is the most respected. "In the economic as well as the ceremonial field the aggressive, competitive, non-co-operative individual is regarded as the aberrant type."[22] It is far easier, however, to label the attitudes of an isolated and primitive Indian culture than to identify complex American society as predominantly co-operative or competitive. Still, it is relatively safe to assume that America balances more heavily on the competitive than the co-operative side. In spite of the co-operative elements in frontier helpfulness, in modern corporate business, in labor unions, and in scientific investigation, American society has, nevertheless, rewarded more consistently the man who rises by his own efforts, who competes vigorously, who is willing to risk loss in the hope of individual gain. Our language teems with competitive symbols: dog eat dog, the ladder of financial success, may the best man win, let the Devil take the hindmost.

A man reared in such a culture, regardless of the extent to which he reviles his environment, will have trouble adjusting himself to the contrasting pattern of a co-operative utopia. In attitudes toward work the colonists frequently evidenced a real conflict between their former and their utopian standards. Wooster believed that one of Llano's greatest tasks was the conquest of the employer-employee psychology. Those who have worked under others all their lives, he said, react strangely when the restraint is lifted.[23] Fountain Grove and Point Loma wrought the most evi-

---

[22]*Co-operation and Competition Among Primitive Peoples* (N.Y., 1937), p. 314. For similar ideas see Ruth Benedict, *Patterns of Culture* (Boston, 1934).

[23]"Inside a Co-operative Colony," *Nation*, CXVII (Oct. 10, 1923), 378-80.

dent changes from a conception of work only for self to one of work for the commonweal. They transformed labor into a religious devotion and consequently offered no direct material return. In all the other colonies, counterparts of wages lingered in the form of time-checks or credit accounts. Gerald Geraldson considered his experience at Auburn to have proved that no colony could succeed unless it broke completely with the old way of life, admitted only members who had no possessions whatsoever, and allowed no money to be dispensed within the colony.

The antagonisms which colonists sometimes felt toward economic planning further mirrored the conflict with earlier habits. The Icarian minute books suggest the bitterness of those who are refused new pants or petticoats while other members are granted new boots.[24] In most of the colonies the distribution of clothes and personal effects, either directly or indirectly through credit accounts, was kept as far as possible within the administrative or executive divisions of government, and in the autocratic colonies the decisions of these branches were final. But in the others, individuals could always appeal to the general assembly, and the frequency of the petitions disclosed the extent to which individuals were not yet accustomed to a planned economy.

Most colonies stressed heavily the education of their young and thereby revealed a deep concern for the formation of new psychological and cultural habits. The sectarian colonies sought to indoctrinate their heirs in the new religion, emphasizing the pattern of brotherhood. At Fountain Grove even the separation of children from parents assumed the nature of an educational process to broaden areas of brotherly love. The secular colonies trained their young in co-operative methods and attitudes. It has usually been the case elsewhere in the nation that secular colonies have been more concerned with education than the religious groups. Oneida's comprehensive plan of training, for example, far outstripped the rudimentary nature of Shaker schooling. In California, however, no such pattern emerged. Point Loma developed an

[24]"Procès-Verbaux de l'Assemblée Generale de la Communauté Icarienne," (MS in possession of Mrs. E. B. Mitchell, Pasadena), pp. 84, 193.

excellent system of education, extensive in ages covered and comprehensive in subject matter. But another sectarian colony, Fountain Grove, gave little thought to its school, and what formal instruction the children received was decidedly restricted in scope. The secular colonies, on the other hand, conformed to the larger utopian pattern. They established excellent school systems with experimental features, as at Llano, or they projected educational programs which promised to be outstanding if completed, as at Altruria and Kaweah.

External hostility intensified the cultural conflict. Manifested in its newspapers, the surrounding society often chided and misrepresented the experiments, seized upon the mistakes and emphasized the inadequacies of co-operation. Faced with such criticism, new habits and configurations can endure only if they first have time to solidify, to catch hold firmly. And time the utopias did not have. No one can declare accurately the period necessary for the transformation of patterns of human reaction. Haskell believed the miracle could be achieved in one generation,[25] and he may have been right if the generation were rigidly isolated from contact with the old ways. Laurence Gronlund considered three generations necessary, the first generation training competent people of the second to be the educators of the third.[26] Certainly while continually encountering the former culture and under frequent bombardment from it, a group may require a span considerably longer than a single generation. In this sense, all utopian colonies have fought a losing battle with time. If the new patterns could have been set, the constant conflict with the surrounding society might have been withstood and might even have stimulated growth. The long and successful careers of the Shaker and Ephrata communities in the East might be explained by the fact that changed habits did have time to coalesce. But in California, as so often elsewhere, dispersal came too soon.

What human beings think of events is sometimes a more impor-

[25]Kaweah, *Out West*, XVII (Sept., 1902), 303.

[26]*Co-operative Commonwealth* (Boston, 1884), p. 227.

tant factor in history than the events themselves, and it may be that the reaction of the colonists to the collapse of their experiments has as great a significance as the economic or social analysis of their failure. Almost invariably the colonist retained faith in the co-operative, communitarian ideal, although the specific activities through which he continued to express the ideal varied from social federation to the founding of more colonies. The Kaweahans joined Nationalist and Populist clubs in San Francisco. The Altrurians associated with consumers' co-operatives both before, during, and after their adventure on Mark West Creek. Icarians established co-operative stores in Cloverdale following their experience with the commune, and former Llano colonists vigorously supported the self-help co-operative movement and Upton Sinclair's E.P.I.C. plan during the 1930's.

Furthermore, ex-colonists were characteristically ready to found or join new colonies. Alvin D. Brock, ex-member of Kaweah, projected various utopias near Suisun during the 1890's. James J. Martin, long-time secretary of Kaweah, organized the United Self Helpers in Vancouver, British Columbia, in 1912 and two years later established a co-operative colony in Tasmania. One Llano veteran had participated in seven colonies, an Icarian had lived at four, and the list of men who had survived more than one colony could be extended indefinitely. Ex-Icarians joined the Shakers; Shakers joined Altruria; Theosophists and men from Topolobampo and Equality joined Llano; and even today a group of chronic Llano colonists headed by Walter Millsap plans a new colony under the name Ucopia. Burnette Haskell wrote in 1906, the year before he died, "Damn that old Cause that keeps our consciences working all the time and will not let us sleep and dream in peace."[27]

These are the utopians, "who listen with credulity to the whispers of fancy, and pursue with eagerness the phantoms of hope; who expect that age will perform the promises of youth, and that the deficiencies of the present day will be supplied by the mor-

[27]In Frank Roney, *Frank Roney: ...An Autobiography*, ed. by Ira B. Cross (Berkeley, 1931), pp. xix-xx.

row."[28] In California they have fostered an extraordinary growth of colonies. They have shared ideas with the broader realm of utopianism and with widespread social movements like Nationalism and Christian Socialism. And they have watched their schemes collapse from political, economic, and cultural conflicts which have, even so, left the individual ready to venture anew.

An elderly woman, enthusiastic colonist of a religious utopia, was once explaining the four "neutral points" on the earth's surface from which the salvation of mankind might emerge. Palestine she named first and California second, after which she stopped and her listeners asked eagerly where were the other two. With a distant and transfigured expression, she slowly answered, "No one knows." Similarly the psychological temper of the utopian constantly beckons to an unseen but nevertheless real goal: from one more experiment in community life may yet emerge—like a phoenix, momentarily dusted with the disappointments of the past—a resplendent, reformed mankind gathered in the ideal society.

[28]Samuel Johnson, *History of Rasselas, Prince of Abissinia*, ed. by R. W. Chapman (Oxford, 1927), p. 7.

CHAPTER 10

Bibliographical Note

I. GENERAL BIBLIOGRAPHICAL AIDS

A. *Utopian Colonies in America*

No attempt will be made here to survey the wide and growing body of material on utopian colonies in America, since two recent and comprehensive bibliographies cover the subject most adequately. Arthur E. Bestor, Jr., *Backwoods Utopias: the Sectarian and Owenite Phases of Communitarian Socialism in America, 1663-1829* (Phila., 1950), begins his Bibliographical Essay by evaluating all of, the existing studies of the communitarian movement as a whole. An even more recent bibliography composes the second volume of Donald D. Egbert and Stow Persons, eds., and T. D. Seymour Bassett, bibliographer, *Socialism and American Life* (2 vols., Princeton, 1952). Its listings under "Communitarian Socialism" (II, 94-97) are selective, but nevertheless extensive. Two helpful shorter guides are the bibliography following the excellent article "Communistic Settlements" by Dorothy W. Douglas and Katherine D. Lumpkin in the *Encyclopedia of the Social Sciences* and Joseph W. Eaton and Saul M. Katz, *Research Guide on Co-operative Group Farming, A Research Bibliography on Rural Co-operative Production and Co-operative Communities* (N.Y., 1942).

B. *California: State and County Histories*

Anyone writing of California should be indebted for the insights of Robert Glass Cleland's sound and inspiring histories, most notably *From Wilderness to Empire: A History of California, 1542-1900* (N.Y., 1944) and *California in Our Time: 1900-1940*

(N.Y., 1947). John Walton Caughey's *California* (N.Y., 1940) is also valuable for its lengthy bibliography. From the standpoint of the utopian colonies in their local settings, an indispensable guide is Ethel Blumann and Mabel W. Thomas, eds., *California Local History: A Centennial Bibliography* (Stanford, 1950). Ira B. Cross, *A History of the Labor Movement in California* (Berkeley, 1935) has been particularly valuable for the backgrounds of those colonies springing from labor circles.

Most of California's county histories have steered safely around the probable subscribers' fear of socialism by ignoring utopian colonies entirely. If, however, a county history has proved of any value, it has been listed below as secondary material under the appropriate colony.

II. THE CALIFORNIA UTOPIAS

A. *Fountain Grove*

1. *Sources*

The library and papers of Thomas Lake Harris have been widely scattered since the death of his trusted follower, Kanaye Nagasawa, in 1934. The final disintegration came in 1948 when the remaining books and papers were auctioned in San Francisco to various bookdealers who thereafter sold the collections piecemeal. The most important single accumulation now available is that made by Herbert W. Schneider and deposited as the Thomas Lake Harris Collection in the Columbia University Library. The collection includes copies of almost all of Harris' published books and pamphlets and many unpublished writings. The Thomas Lake Harris Papers at the Library of Congress contain only a few items from Fountain Grove and these deal mostly with esoteric theology.

Thomas Lake Harris wrote at least fifty-four books and pamphlets during his lifetime. Herbert W. Schneider and George Lawton, *A Prophet and a Pilgrim* (N.Y., 1942), pp. 561-63, have listed the greater part of them. From these works the following bear particular reference to Fountain Grove or elucidate aspects of life there: *Battle Bells* (n.p., n.d.); *Brotherhood of the New Life: Its Fact, Law, Method, and Purpose* (Fountain Grove, Calif., 1891); *God's Breath in Man and in Humane Society* (Fountain Grove, 1891); *The Golden Child: A Daily Chronicle:* Part I, *Songs of Fairyland* (n.p., 1878); *The Lord: the Two-in-One, Declared, Manifested and Glorified* (Salem-on-Erie, N. Y., 1876); *Lyra Triumphalis: People Songs, Ballads, and Marches* (Santa Rosa, Calif., 1891); *The New Republic: A Discourse of the Prospects, Dangers, Duties, and Safeties of the Times* (Santa Rosa, 1891).

Arthur A. Cuthbert, a member of the colony and long a follower of Harris, in *The Life and World-work of Thomas Lake Harris, written from Direct Personal Knowledge* (Glasgow, 1909), intimately revealed the thought processes of a Harrisite. Rosa Emerson, also a member, wrote a fictionalized account of life at the Brocton community, *Among the Chosen* (N.Y., 1884).

A contemporary eye-witness description of Harris as a personality in the 1850's can be found in J. Parton, *The Life of Horace Greeley* (N.Y., 1854), pp. 425-27. Edwin Markham, a frequent visitor to Fountain Grove, gave a most sympathetic evaluation of Harris in *California the Wonderful* (N.Y., 1914), pp. 341-49. The Masonic Lodge of Santa Rosa on July 4, 1906, printed a favorable testimonial to the character of Harris; California State Library, "Memorial Pamphlets," Vol. I.

Some of the British members of the sect have described Harris as they knew him and personal experiences in the brotherhood. The most important of these are C. M. Berridge, *Brotherhood of the New Life; an Epitome of the Work and Teaching of Thomas Lake Harris,* by Respiro, pseud., (12 vols., Glasgow, 1896-1917) and William P. Swainson's two eulogistic works: *Thomas Lake Harris: Mad or Inspired?* (Croydon, Eng., 1895) and *Thomas Lake Harris and His Occult Teaching* (London, 1922). The latter was reprinted in G. M. Hort, *et al, Three Famous Occultists* (London, [1939]).

In the Sonoma County Courthouse, Santa Rosa, Recorder's

Office, is the Deed of April 27, 1875, by which Harris purchased the land at Fountain Grove. In the Clerk's Office are the marriage license of Harris and Jane Lee Waring, 1892; a certificate of co-partnership of 1893, indicating the legal status in which Harris left the colony after his departure; and the will of Kanaye Nagasawa, filed March 5, 1934, evidencing the final dismemberment of the estate, which had been kept intact by Nagasawa till this time.

2. *Secondary Material*

Herbert W. Schneider and George Lawton, *A Prophet and a Pilgrim* (N.Y., 1942) is the only scholarly and objective biography of Thomas Lake Harris and Laurence Oliphant. The Appendices include valuable documents concerning the Fountain Grove period. Schneider also wrote the article on Harris in the *DAB*. Margaret O. W. Oliphant, *Memoir of the Life of Laurence Oliphant* (2 vols., N.Y., 1891) is important for the part it played in the life of Harris and also for the reprinting of numerous letters not otherwise available. Margaret Oliphant was Laurence's cousin and strongly biased against Harris. The book created considerable interest on appearance; see, for example, "A Modern Mystic," *Atlantic Monthly*, LXVIII (Sept., 1891), 414-26, and W. F. Barry, "Laurence Oliphant," *Quarterly Review* (London), CLXXIII (Oct., 1891), 392-413. Some shorter accounts with additional details about Harris are James Main Dixon, in *West Coast Magazine*, IX (Nov., 1910), 170-72; Frank Bailey Millard, *History of the San Francisco Bay Region* (3 vols., Chicago, 1924), I, 459; and Vernon L. Parrington, Jr., *American Dreams: A Study of American Utopias* (Providence, 1947), pp. 161, 163-65. For Kanaye Nagasawa see *Who's Who in California* (San Francisco, 1929).

The colony itself is treated briefly in William A. Hinds, *American Communities* (3rd ed., Chicago, 1908); Ernest S. Wooster, *Communities of the Past and Present* (Newllano, La., 1924); Idwal Jones, *Vines in the Sun* (N.Y., 1949); and William S. Bailey, "The Harris Community—Brotherhood of the New Life," *New York History*, XVI (July, 1935), 278-85.

The following county histories have been found particularly useful: J. P. Munro-Frazer, *History of Sonoma County* (San Francisco, 1879), pp. 427-30; and Thomas Jefferson Gregory, *History of Sonoma County, Calif.* (Los Angeles, 1911), pp. 167-68. Two atlases are important for accurate location of the property: *Historical Atlas Map of Sonoma County, Calif.* (Oakland, 1877) and *Illustrated Atlas of Sonoma County, Calif.* (Santa Rosa, 1897).

Since the colony did not publish a newspaper of its own, contemporary newspaper accounts must come from the outside world. The best of these are the Santa Rosa *Press-Democrat* (daily, 1875 to date; titled the Santa Rosa *Daily Democrat* from 1875 to 1896); and the *Sonoma Democrat* (Santa Rosa, weekly, 1857-97). The most complete files are in the Santa Rosa Public Library.

B. *Theosophists at Point Loma*

1. *Sources*

The two works upon which the whole structure of Theosophy rests are Helena Petrovna Blavatsky, *Isis Unveiled* (2 vols., N.Y., 1877) and *The Secret Doctrine* (3 vols., London, 1888-97). Their basic ideas can be more readily digested in such works of later leaders of the movement as Annie Besant, *The Ideals of Theosophy* (Adyar, India, 1912); Annie Besant, "Theosophical Society," in the *Hastings' Encyclopedia of Religion and Ethics*; and Henry Steel Olcott, *Old Diary Leaves: The True Story of the Theosophical Society* (N.Y., 1895). Two articles in which leaders of Theosophy give both doctrine and historical background are H. S. Olcott, "Theosophy and Theosophists," *Overland Monthly* (San Francisco), n.s., XXXVII (May, 1901), 992-98; and Ernest T. Hargrove, "Progress of Theosophy in the United States," *North American Review* (N.Y.), CLXII (June, 1896), 698-704. A good source for the early rise of Theosophy in California is the *New Californian*, a Theosophical monthly published in San Francisco from 1891-94; partial file in the

Bancroft Library. A biased work, which many Theosophists consider the best biography of Mme. Blavatsky, is Charles J. Ryan, *H. P. Blavatsky and the Theosophical Movement: A Brief Historical Sketch* (Pt. Loma, Calif., 1937); actually the book takes on the nature of a source since it was written by a member of the community at Point Loma and is a fine illustration of the idolization of Blavatsky among Theosophists there.

As for the Point Loma community, the basic collection is the Archives of the Theosophical Society itself, the lineal descendant of Katherine Tingley's Universal Brotherhood, headquarters of which are now in Pasadena. The Leader, Mr. James A. Long, and his assistant, Miss Grace F. Knoche, were most kind in hunting for and allowing the use of any specific material which I requested.

Compared with Madame Blavatsky or Mrs. Besant, Katherine Tingley wrote little; several of her volumes are no more than collections of but three or four speeches. Of these, her most important works are: *The Life at Point Loma* (Pt. Loma, 1908); *The Gods Await* (Pt. Loma, 1926), especially useful for autobiographical portions; *The Voice of the Soul* (Pt. Loma, 1928); and *The Wine of Life* (Pt. Loma, 1925). One of the members of the community, Lillian Whiting, wrote a decidedly sympathetic, but useful evaluation of *Katherine Tingley: Theosophist and Humanitarian* (Pt. Loma, 1919). A record of Katherine Tingley's most important court action will be found in Katherine Tingley vs. Times-Mirror Co., Transcript of Appeal from Superior Court of San Diego County, Aug. 15, 1904, California Supreme Court, Los Angeles.

The periodicals printed at Point Loma give a fuller picture of life in the colony than any other source. The most important of these, a lavishly illustrated monthly, assumed several titles but was known for the longest period as the *Theosophical Path*. It began publication in New York and moved to Point Loma as the *New Century* (1897-1903), became the *New Century Path* (1903-06), the *Century Path* (1907-11), and later the *Theosophical Path* (1911-35). In 1935 it was superseded by the

Theosophical Forum, which had been published concurrently at Point Loma, monthly, from 1929. The *Forum* lasted till the end of the Point Loma experience and was continued thereafter in Covina. *Lucifer*, a reincarnation of Mme. Blavatsky's London journal, was published at Point Loma from 1930 to 1935 and the *Raja Yoga Messenger*, devoted almost wholly to the school, from 1904 to 1929. The Bancroft Library has an extensive file of these periodicals and complete sets can be found at the Theosophical headquarters in Pasadena.

A number of outsiders wrote eye-witness accounts of visits to Point Loma. The most reliable of these, because apparently the most unbiased, is Ray Stannard Baker, "An Extraordinary Experiment in Brotherhood," *American Magazine*, LXIII (Jan., 1907), 227-40. Charles F. Lummis wrote in praise of the community after his visit there and printed many of his own snapshots in "In the Lion's Den," *Out West*, XVII (Dec., 1902), 736-38, and "Those Terrible Mysteries," *Out West*, XVIII (Jan., 1903), 35-48. Other visitors included: Felix J. Koch, "With the Theosophists at Point Loma," *Overland Monthly*, LXII (Oct., 1913), 340-44; Karl H. von Wiegand, "Mystics, Babies, and Bloom," *Sunset*, XXIII (Aug., 1909), 115-26; and Bertha Damaris Knobe, "The Point Loma Community," *Munsey's Magazine*, XXIX (June, 1903), 357-63.

2. Secondary Material

Ernest Sutherland Bates has excellent articles on Katherine Tingley, Helena Blavatsky, and Henry Steel Olcott in the *DAB*. Alvin Boyd Kuhn, *Theosophy: A Modern Revival of Ancient Wisdom* (N.Y., 1930) includes only a small section on the California experience, but it is one of the fullest pictures of the whole subject available. Emmett Alwyn Greenwalt, "The Point Loma Community in California" (Ph.D. dissertation, U.C.L.A., 1949), is undoubtedly the best work yet done on Point Loma.

No one working on any subject dealing with the San Diego area can fail to be grateful to the San Diego Public Library for its file of the daily San Diego *Union* (1871 to date) and its Index

to parts of this file. For the most part, events at the community
received sympathetic treatment at the hands of the *Union* and
were reported in some detail.

C. *Icaria Speranza*

1. *Sources*

Of the newspapers associated with Icaria Speranza, Jules
Leroux's *L'Etoile des Pauvres et des Souffrants*, published monthly and irregularly at St. Helena, Calif., from January through
July, 1881, and at Cloverdale, Calif., from August, 1881, to
October, 1883, is most directly concerned with the colony. A
nearly complete file is in the Bancroft Library. It was a descendant of Leroux's earlier journals: *L'Etoile du Kansas* (Neuchatel,
Nemaha Co., Kansas, 1874-76); and *L'Etoile du Kansas et de
l'Iowa* (Corning, Adams Co., Iowa, 1877-80). *La Jeune Icarie*,
published weekly at Corning, Iowa, from 1878 to 1880, provides
an indispensable background for the Iowa group from which
the California colony grew. *La Revue Icarienne*, published
monthly at Corning, Iowa, from 1878 to 1888, was the organ
of the group which had withdrawn to New Icaria and often
pointedly ignored the former comrades in California. Partial
files of both *La Jeune Icarie* and *La Revue Icarienne* are on
microfilm in the Huntington Library.

Some mention should be made of the ideological backgrounds
of the colony. Etienne Cabet's *Voyage en Icarie, Roman Philoso-
phique et Social* first appeared in two volumes, Paris, 1840, but
the 3rd edition, 1848, had the widest circulation. The Macdonald
MS. in the Yale University Library includes (pp. 141-87) a
personal interview with Cabet in addition to such printed sources
as Cabet's *History of Icaria* (1852), the *Conditions of Admission*
(Nauvoo, 1854), and the *Constitution of 1850*.

Miss Alice M. Dehay of Cloverdale, living in the main house
which the colony built, has photographs of the colonists and
a few manuscripts of her mother, Marie Leroux Dehay, wife
of Armand. Professor Ernest Marchand of San Diego State

College, San Diego, has a small but valuable collection of letters to and from his father, Alexis Marchand, at least thirty of which deal with the California period.

A most valuable source for the story of the Corning episode is the collection of letters, papers, and documents in the possession of Mrs. Eva Bettannier Mitchell of Pasadena, California. Her father was the last president of the colony in Iowa and consequently such important items as the minutes of the General Assembly at New Icaria have come into her possession. Also important for details of everyday life in an Icarian community is Mrs. Marie Marchand Ross's autobiography of her life at New Icaria, *Child of Icaria* (n.p., n.d.; [c. 1938]).

2. *Secondary Material*

Histories of the Icarian communities which have included short sections on the California group must begin with the pioneering work of Albert Shaw, *Icaria: A Chapter in the History of Communism* (N.Y., 1884). Shaw, later editor of the *Review of Reviews*, wrote from the sources and, particularly important from the standpoint of California, included letters from the California members and his own estimates of some of the personalities there. Mrs. Marion Tinling, formerly of the Huntington Library, was kind enough to let me read her unpublished manuscript, "Icaria: A Communist Colony in America" (1948), which, however, includes only a short section on California. Jules Prudhommeaux's extensive work *Icarie et son Fondateur Etienne Cabet* (Paris, 1907) reprints in the appendix several documents which are not available elsewhere.

For works on Icarian history which do not necessarily include California, see the exhaustive bibliography in Jules Prudhommeaux, *Icarie*, pp. xiii-xl.

An undocumented, but lively, account of the California colony is Jehanne Bietry Salinger's "A French Chapter in Social Experiment," in *Le 'Guide' des Commerçants Français en Californie* (San Francisco, 1939); in possession of Miss Alice M. Dehay, Cloverdale. The only adequate file of the Cloverdale *Weekly*

Reveille for the nineteenth century is the badly broken collection in the Bancroft Library.

D. *Kaweah*

1. *Sources*

The Bancroft Library has recently reassorted its collection on the Kaweah Colony under new headings for the two principal men represented in the collection: Burnette G. Haskell and James J. Martin. These papers constitute an enormous collection of letters, diaries, ledgers, and pamphlets, indispensable to a history of Kaweah.

A smaller repository of documents which bear chiefly on the relations of the government to the colony is in the Historical File, Park Naturalist's office, Sequoia National Park. Reports of special investigators to the United States government are found in the *Congressional Record,* 52nd Congress, 2nd Session, Vol. XXIV, Part II, p. 1471, and *Senate Reports,* 52nd Congress, 2nd Session, Vol. I, No. 1248.

The Philip Winser MS. in the Huntington Library recounts in detail life and events at the colony through the eyes of a member. Unfortunately it was written in 1931, long after the experience. Winser wrote an earlier, shorter piece, "Sketch of Kaweah," in the *Altrurian,* July 15, 1895.

The colony newspaper, the *Commonwealth* (San Francisco and/or Kaweah, 1886-1892) can be found in the Bancroft Library, where only scattered issues are lacking, and in the Tulare County Library, Visalia, California. The Bancroft Library holds a nearly complete file of *Truth,* the paper which Haskell edited in San Francisco from 1882 to 1884. During this same period Haskell wrote an Introduction and Appendices for A. J. Starkweather and S. Robert Wilson, *Socialism* (N.Y., 1884) which throw light on the relations of his I. W. A. with the wider socialist world.

Eight propaganda pamphlets (catalogued as "Kaweah Co-operative Colony, Pamphlets relating to, 1886-89") are in the

Library of the University of California at Los Angeles. Martin and Haskell both wrote glowing prospectuses of Kaweah in the *Nationalist*: Burnette G. Haskell, "A Plan of Action," *Nationalist*, II (Dec., 1889), 30-32; James J. Martin, "A Co-operative Commonwealth: the Kaweah Colony," *ibid.*, I (Oct., 1889), 204-208.

Professor William Carey Jones of the University of California, after visits to the colony and correspondence with its leaders, wrote sympathetic opinions in "The Kaweah Experiment in Co-operation," *Quarterly Journal of Economics*, VI (Oct., 1891), 47-85. Another visitor, George W. Stewart, wrote severely and critically: "History of the Kaweah Colony, 1885-89" (compiled from articles written by Stewart for the Visalia *Delta*, Nov. and Dec., 1891), manuscript in Tulare Free Library, Tulare, California.

2. Secondary Material

Ira B. Cross, *A History of the Labor Movement in California* (Berkeley, 1935), a scholarly and readable work, is the best introduction to backgrounds from which Kaweah sprang. Chester M. Destler in *American Radicalism, 1865-1901: Essays and Documents* (New London, Conn., 1946), pp. 79-103, presents interesting comments on Haskell and reprints a letter which Haskell sent to J. A. Labadie and August Spies in 1883 proposing union between anarchists and socialists.

An unpublished manuscript by Herbert L. Junep, "A Chronological History of the Sequoia National Park and Vicinity," in the office of the Park Naturalist, Sequoia National Park, deals directly with Kaweah on pp. 125-222.

The following accounts of the colony reflect decidedly sympathetic opinions: Carey McWilliams, *Factories in the Field* (Boston, 1935), pp. 28-29, 39-47; Charles H. Shinn, "Co-operation on the Pacific Coast," in *History of Co-operation in the United States* (Johns Hopkins Univ. Studies in Historical and Political Science, Baltimore, 1888), pp. 447-81; Edward B. Payne, "Lessons from Kaweah," *Altrurian*, Dec. 21, 1895. The

latter is based on an interview with J. G. Wright, a former
member of Kaweah. For more objective studies see Ruth R.
Lewis, "Kaweah: An Experiment in Co-operative Colonization,"
Pacific Historical Review, XVII (Nov., 1948), 429-41, and
Robert Hine, "A California Utopia: 1885-1890," *Huntington
Library Quarterly*, XI (August, 1948), 387-405.

E. *Altruria*

1. *Sources*

Of the principal utopian colonies in this study, Altruria has
left the least tangible record of its existence. The colony's weekly
newspaper, the *Altrurian* (1894-96), a complete file of which
is in the Bancroft Library, provides the most important single
source. It was edited by Edward B. Payne and began publication
in Berkeley on Oct. 6, 1894, moving to the colony after Nov.
22, 1894, and publishing there weekly till Feb. 22, 1896. It became a monthly in May, 1896, and ceased publication in November of that year. In the same covers with the *Altrurian*, the
Bancroft Library has bound a series of significant documents:
"Altruria Community: Constitution of the Grand Council and
Constitution of the Subordinate Councils" (printed also in
Altrurian, Feb. 18, 1895); "Altruria Community: Application
for Membership" (blank); and two printed broadsides describing the community for propaganda purposes.

The works of Edward Biron Payne are slight and consist
chiefly of magazine articles. Most significant from the standpoint
of the colony are "Altruria," *American Magazine of Civics*, VI
(Feb., 1895), 168-71; and "The Socialist's Answer," in a sym-
posium, "What Shall Society Do to Be Saved?" *Overland
Monthly*, XXXV (June, 1900), 530-34. Other works of Payne
which delineate his character are: "Lilies and Men," *Overland
Monthly*, XXXV (April, 1900), 349-52; "The Inspired Scrip-
ture" and "The Drill of a Soldier" in *Pamphlets by California
Authors*, Vol. III (n.p., n.d.), University of California Library;
"To the Immortal" (pamphlet, n.p., 1895), University of Cali-

fornia Library; *Waste Philosophy* (Berkeley, Calif., 1892); "Spectres on the Overland Trail," *Overland Monthly,* XIV (Dec., 1889), 654-57; "The City of Education," *ibid.,* XXXIV (Oct., Nov., 1899), 353-61, 448-55; *The Soul of Jack London* (Kingsport, Tenn., 1933). The latter was published posthumously and includes a revealing preface concerning Payne by his widow.

The best account of the colony by a visitor, who was in fact so frequent a visitor and so sympathetic a participant that he could almost be termed a member, is Morrison I. Swift, "Altruria in California," *Overland Monthly,* XXIX (June, 1897), 643-45. The By-laws of the Altruria Co-operative Union of Oakland, Calif. (Oakland, 1895) have been preserved in the Bancroft Library. The book from which the colony took its name and many of its ideas, William Dean Howells, *A Traveler from Altruria* (N.Y., 1894), was first printed in *Cosmopolitan* magazine in monthly installments between November, 1892, and October, 1893. Ambrose Bierce's bitter comments on Altruria appeared in the San Francisco *Examiner,* Oct. 21, 1894.

In the Sonoma County Courthouse, Clerk's Office, will be found the Articles of Incorporation of Altruria Association, 1895 (Document No. 437); and the By-laws of Altruria Association, 1896 (Document No. 440).

2. Secondary Material

The best studies of the religious background from which the colony grew are James Dombrowski, *The Early Days of Christian Socialism in America* (N.Y., 1936) and Charles H. Hopkins, *The Rise of the Social Gospel in American Protestantism: 1865-1915* (New Haven, 1940).

In the local histories only Ernest Finley, *History of Sonoma County, Calif.* (Santa Rosa, 1937); Thomas Gregory, *History of Sonoma County, Calif.* (Los Angeles, 1911); *Illustrated Atlas of Sonoma County, Calif.* (Santa Rosa, 1897); F. M. Husted's *Oakland, Alameda and Berkeley Directory* for 1892-93 and for 1896 (San Francisco, 1892, 1895) are helpful.

F. *Llano*

1. *Sources*

Two periodicals were published at the colony: the *Llano Colonist* (weekly) and the *Western Comrade* (monthly). The *Llano Colonist* had three distinct lives: at Llano, Calif., from 1916 to 1919 (the few remaining members continued its publication after the majority had moved to Louisiana); in Newllano, La., from 1921 to 1937, during which time there were also parallel but sporadic runs of papers published under the same name by sympathizers of the colony in Berkeley, Calif., and Washington, D.C.; and finally a short series of fourteen issues published by ex-colonists in Los Angeles during 1947. Files for the paper during the 1916-19 period, the most relevant to the colony's California days, will be found at the State Historical Society, Madison, Wisconsin, in the Los Angeles Public Library, and in the personal possession of Walter Millsap, Los Angeles. The *Western Comrade* began publication in Los Angeles in April, 1913, edited by Stanley B. Wilson and Chester M. Wright. Franklin E. Wolfe became its editor in July, 1914, with Job Harriman, managing editor. After Wolfe joined Llano in June, 1916, the journal was published at the colony. It moved to Newllano, La., in Nov., 1917, where it was issued till March-April, 1918, when it was re-named the *Internationalist* for two issues and then allowed to die. The California State Library has a complete file.

An "Agreement to Purchase Stock and Agreement of Employment," Dec. 1, 1916, signed by Job Harriman and W. A. Engle is in the Huntington Library. The colony published for propaganda purposes a twenty-four page book of pictures, one copy of which has been preserved in the Library of the University of California at Los Angeles: *Llano Viewbook* (Llano, Calif., 1917).

The most prolific writer of personal experience at the colony was Ernest S. Wooster. His comments were colored by his deep sympathy with the aims and purposes, but he had a sense of humor and fairness which allowed him occasionally to describe the seamy side. His *Communities of the Past and Present* (New-llano, La., 1924) has a long section on Llano and also includes a very important introduction by Job Harriman. The latter, written the year before Harriman's death, indicates the changes of opinion which Harriman underwent after his years of experience with utopia. Wooster's other articles appeared in *Sunset*, LIII (July, 1924), 21-23, 80, 81-82; (Aug., 1924), 21-23, 59-60; (Sept., 1924), 30-33, 75-80; and *Nation*, CXVII (Oct. 10, 1923), 378-80.

Several accounts written in Louisiana are, nevertheless, important for the period in California because they describe members who had come from California and report conversations with them. The most important of these are Robert Carlton Brown, *Can We Co-operate?* (Pleasant Plains, N.Y., 1940) and Alexander James McDonald, *The Llano Co-operative Colony and What it Taught* (Leesville, La., 1950). Brown writes in a supercilious manner which is frequently irritating; McDonald maintains a less emotional and less dogmatic approach. McDonald, however, is attempting to justify his own actions against George Pickett in the final dissolution. Sid Young, a member, discusses the disintegration in Louisiana with occasional backward glances at California in *The Crisis in Llano Colony, 1935-36: An Epic Story* (Los Angeles, 1936).

A valuable source of information has been Mr. Walter Millsap of Los Angeles, who joined the colony in July, 1916, and early gained a leading position in its councils, which he maintained till he left the Louisiana site late in 1919. He has been kind enough to criticize an early draft of the chapter on Llano in the light of his own experiences.

A. R. Clifton, although not a member of the colony, did conduct a firsthand study on the colony's grounds: "History of the Communistic Colony Llano del Rio," Historical Society of Southern California, *Annual Publications*, XI (1918), 80-90.

Job Harriman himself wrote very little. The record of his debate with Daniel DeLeon in New Haven on November 25, 1900, and one of his pamphlets, *The Class War in Idaho* (N.Y.,

1900), are preserved in the Yale University Library. An article written during his candidacy for mayor of Los Angeles, "What's the Matter with L.A.?" appeared in *Collier's* XLVIII (Dec. 2, 1911), 28. Two of his pieces in the *Western Comrade* reveal his concern for public ownership and his earliest hopes for Llano: "Making Dreams Come True," *Western Comrade*, I (May, 1913), 54-56; and "The Gateway to Freedom," *ibid.*, II (June, 1914), 6-9, 24-25.

Discussions of Harriman by his associates are in Thomas W. Williams, "A Short History of the Socialist Movement in California," Los Angeles *Citizen*, Sept. 1, 1911; and Morris Hillquit, *History of Socialism in the United States* (N.Y., 1903), p. 329. Colleagues during the McNamara trial made favorable comments about Harriman in subsequent writings: Clarence Darrow, *The Story of My Life* (N.Y., 1932), pp. 175, 184; and Lincoln Steffens, *Autobiography* (2 vols., N.Y., 1931), II, 666, 679, 688. On the other hand, William J. Burns, the detective hired by the *Times* after the bombing, gives a decidedly unsympathetic picture of the man in *The Masked War* (N.Y., 1913), pp. 94, 275, 284. The best source on the trial is the voluminous transcription of United States vs. Frank N. Ryan, *et al*, Indianapolis, Indiana, October 3–December 17, 1912; Huntington Library MS. 1152.

2. *Secondary Material*

The Bureau of Labor Statistics of the U. S. Department of Labor twice included reports on Llano in its *Monthly Review*: "The Llano del Rio Co-operative Colony," *Monthly Review*, II (Jan., 1916), 19-23; and "Llano Co-operative Colony," *ibid.*, XXXII (May, 1931), 101-109. A more recent investigation produced a short "Report on the Llano del Rio Co. of Nevada by John B. Pollard, State Farm Debtor Supervisor for the State of Louisiana, 1939"; copy in University of California Library at Los Angeles.

Broader studies which have looked sympathetically on Llano include Charles Gide, *Communist and Co-operative Colonies* (London, 1930; translated by Ernest F. Row from Gide's *Les*

Colonies Communistes et Coopératives, [Paris, 1928]), pp. 203-208; and Henrik F. Infield, *Co-operative Communities at Work* (N.Y., 1945), pp. 37-52. A more objective but little documented view is taken by Victor F. Calverton in *Where Angels Dared to Tread* (Indianapolis, 1941), pp. 364-66.

Louis Adamic looked askance at Harriman's relations with the McNamara case, suggesting that he may have been more implicated in the dynamiting than is usually supposed: *Dynamite: the Story of Class Violence in America* (2nd ed., rev. with Bibliography, N.Y., 1934), pp. 207 ff., 211, 218, 220, 233, 242. Charles Yale Harrison pictures Harriman as considerably less devious and more reliable: *Clarence Darrow* (N.Y., 1931), pp. 148, 151, 158, 172. At the time of Harriman's candidacy for mayor of Los Angeles, the Los Angeles *Times*, reflecting its traditional hostility to labor unions and radical groups, printed great numbers of disparaging comments about Harriman: Dec. 1, 2, 3, 4, and 7, 1911. Obituaries for Harriman can be found in the Los Angeles *Times*, Oct. 28 and Oct. 30, 1925, and in the San Francisco *Chronicle* and the San Francisco *Examiner*, both for October 28, 1925.